Outstanding
School Administrators

Their Keys to Success

*Frederick C. Wendel, Fred A. Hoke,
and Ronald G. Joekel*

PRAEGER

Westport, Connecticut
London

Library of Congress Cataloging-in-Publication Data

Wendel, Frederick C.
 Outstanding school administrators : their keys to success /
Frederick C. Wendel, Fred A. Hoke, and Ronald G. Joekel.
  p. cm.
 Includes bibliographical references and index.
 ISBN 0–275–94822–6 (alk. paper)
  1. School administrators—United States. 2. School management and
organization—United States—Philosophy. 3. Educational leadership—
United States. I. Hoke, Fred A. II. Joekel, Ronald G. III. Title.
LB2831.82.W45 1996
371.2'01'0973—dc20   95–23208

British Library Cataloguing in Publication Data is available.

Library of Congress Catalog Card Number: 95–23208
ISBN: 0–275–94822–6

First published in 1996

Praeger Publishers, 88 Post Road West, Westport, CT 06881
An imprint of Greenwood Publishing Group, Inc.

Printed in the United States of America

The paper used in this book complies with the
Permanent Paper Standard issued by the National
Information Standards Organization (Z39.48–1984).

10 9 8 7 6 5 4 3 2 1

Copyright Acknowledgment

The authors and publisher gratefully acknowledge permission to quote from the following:

Wendel, F. C., Hoke, F. A., & Joekel, R. G. (1993). Project success: Outstanding principals speak
out. *The Clearing House, 67*(1), 52–54.

This book is dedicated to the school administrators who shared their keys to success.

The authors also express their appreciation to their wives for their support and understanding during the preparation of this book.

Roxie Rosenthal who prepared the manuscript for publication is gratefully acknowledged for her dedication, thoroughness, and patience.

CONTENTS

INTRODUCTION

This book is a tribute to seekers of success—to those who want to plumb the depths of the human spirit. The book is a guide to those tired of studying disease to discover a cure. The premise of the book is that to become healthy, individuals must pattern the ways of the healthy. To be successful, individuals must study and implement the habits and attitudes of the successful.

All educators, administrators included, must improve. Administrators must bring the best of everything into their lives to make substantial progress and to tap their potential. The best part of education is taking off the shackles that have bound us—recognizing that much of what we have learned and become has been put upon us by well-meaning friends, teachers, and parents. But something inside each of us continues to question that information. Now after years of dissecting industry, government, and the schools, we want to know those characteristics of administrators who really are making a difference—who have peeled back some of the outmoded concepts and revealed the core essence of successful school administrators.

In the 1980s, especially after the publication of *A Nation at Risk*, which lamented a "rising tide of mediocrity" in schools, negative criticism of education, public education, educators, and administrators abounded. Not everyone thought that the first light of doomsday was dawning upon public education in America, however. How could the good news be broadcast as well as the bad news? To share the good news of what was transpiring in education, we launched Project Success. Project Success was conceived to tell the good news of what happens in schools, to relate what administrators are doing to enrich the lives of students and members of their communities, and to reveal the self-reflections of outstanding school administrators.

The three of us wrote to dozens of individuals in leadership positions in schools, state education agencies, professional organizations, and universities to obtain the names of successful administrators. The responses to our request for names and addresses of successful administrators were encouraging as we received the names of over 1,000 school administrators. Next, we wrote all nominees, explained the purpose of Project Success, indicated that someone had nominated them as outstanding, and made our request. We simply asked, "Why do you believe that you were nominated as an outstanding school administrator?" and "What attributes do you exhibit that have encouraged other educational leaders to look to you for outstanding leadership?" In many cases, respondents were contacted a second time to expand upon their original comments. Eventually, 491 administrators answered our request. Their responses filled six notebooks and provided intimate reflections on the lives of outstanding administrators. Through a lengthy process, their responses were categorized, ultimately into eleven factors that comprise the basis of this book.

In some cases, respondents completed and returned a "Release for Research and Publication" form that gave us permission to use their names in publications. Hence their names, administrative positions, and states are provided. Others did not return a completed "Release for Research and Publication" form. Their identities are masked, with reference made to them only by administrative position and state.

Reading the responses was enjoyable, ennobling, and uplifting. Reading and re-reading the responses convinced us that outstanding school administrators were identified through Project Success, that good things were happening in schools, and that administrators made a difference in the lives of students in their schools.

We bring you the insights of men and women who have analyzed themselves and decided to apply all their resources to their work and their lives to increase their effectiveness and their impact upon others who journey with them on the road to success.

A book about successful administrators interests many readers. Some want to know about interesting people. Some will want to know what insurmountable odds these people have overcome to accomplish something that had dramatic impact upon others. Some readers will want to see how they might duplicate successes of others in their own professional lives. And others will want to reaffirm for themselves that they demonstrate these characteristics and can achieve the same degree and kind of success if they apply the lessons of successful people to their own lives.

If you want to improve your school, your profession, your professional life, your professional role, your life, and your community, we suggest that you study the insights offered by the administrators interviewed here.

If you are a parent or guardian of school-age children, see if your school administrators exhibit these characteristics. If they do, gather your fellow parents and guardians and recognize these outstanding educators publicly. They are making an inestimable impact on the future success of children and youth.

If administrators and other educators are not as effective as they might be, make a copy of this book available to them. Encourage them to set an example for themselves and their students. And then celebrate this new dedication to personal and professional renewal.

1

EDUCATIONAL
PHILOSOPHY

This chapter presents statements of educational philosophy made by participants in Project Success. The statements are representative of the beliefs, values, and positions successful administrators espouse. As you read through the comments, you will note that many different topics are addressed and that no single set of ideas emerges. The world of education is broad enough to accommodate divergent views, and perhaps only extreme views would be unacceptable. For example, educators might find the statement "I believe that boys should not be taught to sew" a little odd but not repugnant. Statements about more compelling issues, however, can divide faculties, educators from their critics, and members of one camp from another. You may find few new or startling ideas in this chapter, but you may be struck by the clarity of thought, the intensity of belief, and the firmness with which administrators hold onto their beliefs, values, and principles.

The administrators who responded to Project Success were not asked, directly or indirectly, to express their philosophical values, views, and beliefs. They were asked to write what they believed contributed to their success as school administrators. In a follow-up letter, administrators were asked to expand upon their statements, and many did so.

How, then, were their values, views, and beliefs categorized? First, their responses were placed, alphabetically, into six notebooks. Second, each response was read and statements of belief were identified. Statements were screened with a definite principle in mind: "I believe . . ." and similarly worded statements were considered to be statements of educational philosophy. Thus, emphasis was placed upon assertions of one's personal beliefs. Third, quotations of beliefs were transcribed onto a disk file and coded with an index entry. Finally, the index entries were categorized under several broad headings and incorporated into the text of this chapter. Consequently, you may or may not agree with the placement of some comments in a category; however, you do have the opportunity to review, word by word, the written responses of those administrators who participated in Project Success. In some cases, the identity of respondents is noted, as these individuals signed a release form for such a purpose. For those administrators who did not sign and return a release statement for the publication of their names and positions, a masked reference is given, for example, a middle-level principal in a state.

The bulk of this chapter consists of word-by-word quotations of school administrators identified by their peers as highly successful. We hope their words not only inspire you to more productive measures and success but also encourage you to draft personal statements of belief that undergird your values, thoughts, words, and actions.

CREDOS

Several respondents wrote extensive comments about their educational philosophy. Note how often the phrase "I believe" is used as an indication of personal identification with a belief statement. In many instances, "I" is a word to avoid using, but in expressing one's educational philosophy, "I believe" is a sign of depth of feeling about and commitment to a principle of personal importance.

I Believe

A high school principal from South Carolina wrote her set of educational values as follows:

> I believe, and hope, that I practice the following: Students are important people in our business, and I must therefore be an advocate for students. I must take risks for students on behalf of improved student learning. I must maintain integrity in all that I do. I must work harder than my staff. I must have and maintain high expectations for all, including myself. I must treat all people in a fair, caring way. I must care about my own professional development and the professional development of staff. I must build leadership in the people with whom I work. I must be tolerant of others' views and opinions and open to compromise, but I must never sacrifice my principles and values. I must be a leader and a team player. I must be open to change and help to create a climate for change in the school. I must maintain a healthy sense of self and a "gigantic" sense of humor. I must take this business seriously, but I *must not* take myself too seriously.

A superintendent from Arizona offered what he termed "philosophical constructs." Although he does not preface his remarks with "I believe," his statements contain bits of advice about numerous topics that could begin with such a phrase as "I believe that school administrators should"

1. Make those decisions that are driven by that which will best meet the needs of children.
2. Select those staff members who share the commitment and are willing to work together and to best serve.
3. Be available and listen carefully to those seeking audience.
4. Be unswayed by recognition, honors, and praise.
5. Hold firm to basic beliefs but be slow to invoke personal standards on others.
6. Be honest intellectually, morally, and professionally.
7. Consider every person at least an equal and elevate those who struggle to their highest capacity.
8. Remember that schools exist only to serve children.
9. Empower and enable board members so they prosper in achieving agreed-upon educational goals.
10. Be faithful to your promises [spouse].
11. Search for strategies that will strengthen school services.
12. Provide service to the profession and to the community beyond your paid assignment.
13. Work hard and study always.
14. Maintain good health.
15. Be happy.

A middle school principal from Iowa expressed his beliefs tersely:

I believe in

- Discipline—for students and staff alike.
- Fairness—equal treatment to all.
- Safe and progressive learning environment.
- Listening to staff, parents, and students. I believe we had site-based management long before anybody heard of it.
- Community involvement—get the community involved with your school and yourself involved in the community.
- Set an example for staff and students.
- Be an educational advocate in society.
- Professional readings—read *everything* you can on education, the future and so on, and get involved with your associations.
- Be willing to change or modify one's thinking or beliefs.

From Kentucky, a director of school relations provided her three main points about principles for operating schools successfully.

My beliefs about running a successful school include the following: (1) The principal must not only be knowledgeable about instruction but must be a leader in his or her own right. As a leader, a principal will set the tone for the school, articulate goals, and have good communication and interpersonal skills. (2) A school leader must also take the time to involve others in making decisions. More is likely to be accomplished when the implementers are involved in making the decisions. Giving praise and recognition for a job well done is always important. Being a supporter for your employees and showing that you value them is important in building pride in one's accomplishments. (3) A successful school leader must have high moral standards, integrity, and be viewed as fair and trustworthy. These characteristics in concert with appropriate skills and high standards lead to being a successful and respected school administrator.

Did you notice that both the high school principal and the superintendent placed the interests of students first in their comments? The middle school principal and director of school relations, by comparison, chose different approaches to revealing their beliefs and structuring their statements. Yet all four administrators succinctly stated the beliefs that drove their practices.

An assistant superintendent from Nebraska indicated that his educational values affected his actions.

I possess strong educational values that I portray by both example and in written and oral communications. These values are based on the belief that all students can and should be successful. In fact, the primary mission of public education is to make certain all students do succeed. I approach my job as a school administrator as one of service. I serve the community and students. This means working extra hours not only on the job but in numerous community organizations. I am available to visit and consult with any interested party.

Holding Fast

How important is having a set of beliefs such as the preceding ones? A superintendent from Kansas remarked about holding fast to one's beliefs.

Some qualities I value: Know what you believe and don't heed those who will attack your sense of focus, direction, and vision as if it were ego or arrogance. At the same time, don't let your ego keep you from learning from anyone. Maintain a balance between your ambiguity factor (ability to live with the unsolved problem) and a strong gestalt (drive to complete a task) . . . . Have a strong work ethic . . . value productivity. Enjoy (even relish) the process of change. Be the keeper of the values. Know what is important to the organization and be willing to make some personal sacrifice.

The Value of Public Education

How do you feel about the attacks upon education in general, public education specifically, and administrators in particular? The concern about continued criticism of education and educators was the impetus for Project Success. Fortunately, many individuals in prominent positions have unwavering beliefs about one of the cornerstones of American democracy and prompted this response from a superintendent in California.

I am told I have several skills and attributes that help me succeed as a public school administrator. First, I am strongly committed to public education. I believe that an effective system of public schools is absolutely essential to maintaining a free and productive society. I want to make every contribution I can to improving American public education.

Enthusiasm about public education was transmitted by a superintendent from Oregon.

I have often said that being a superintendent has to be about the best job anyone could want. You get to do more interesting things with more people than I ever imagined, and best of all the cause is right. My enthusiasm for school administration and public education has increasingly heightened. Public education has been an awesome experiment and has, of course, been a cornerstone of America's development and I appreciate that. More appreciated is the opportunity for the future. American public education is truly undergoing a paradigm shift as evidenced by global influences, demographic changes, societal demands, school choice, vouchers, and changing expectations. What an exciting time! The paradigm I refer to centers on the necessity to move to a broadened sense of community. The school leader has an expanded community responsibility to rally and facilitate the entire community toward agreed-upon goals. The leader must organize and lead a quality school system, but societal demands and the ability to respond both require an end to isolationism or "living in our own world." I believe that school leaders must be active, visible, and involved throughout the community. Beyond public relations and/or elections as motivators, this involvement of school leaders should be focused toward seeking out partnerships to bring the schools and our mutual concerns into "their worlds." I believe that as an articulate, knowledgeable, spokesman for education who also demonstrates an understanding of business, economic development, and social and community needs, I have been able to gain support for schools and also strengthen the position of the schools within the community. That is the reason for my community involvement, that plus a personal belief about the requirements of responsible citizenship.

Cynthia F. Grennan (personal communication, March 5, 1992), a superintendent of schools, focused upon the potential of education. She incorporated many "I believe" statements into her expressions of the importance of quality education for students and society.

Education perpetuates a progressive, productive society, an investment for the future that must involve all of us. Students, parents, teachers, counselors, and administrators, working together, must strive to involve business, industry, and the community. We who are devoted to progress in education must diligently pursue the belief that all children can learn. We also must accept the challenge to provide resources that ensure quality education for all students. I maintain that society has a responsibility to monitor the quality of schools. I believe that clear vision of educational excellence has to be in place to enable personnel and students to understand their mission and role in the continuing pursuit of excellence. We need to teach them all the skills possible for living in our complex global society. And it is our duty to empower our students with positive attitudes and an understanding that learning is a lifelong process.

Notice how an associate superintendent from Nebraska related her set of beliefs to her actions. Do deeply held beliefs guide one's actions more firmly and focused than ones that are less clearly stated? As you review her set of beliefs, compare your own beliefs with hers, not for the purpose of determining whose set of beliefs is better but, rather, to determine how cogently yours can be stated.

I act from a set of beliefs that undergird my work as a school administrator: I believe that all persons have innate worth and value as human beings; I believe that all children can learn; I believe that leadership is a participatory process, not a spotlight; I believe that all educators want to be as effective as they can be; I believe we are involved in the most important adventure of all—the growth and development of young people. From those beliefs, I try to follow a set of practices. I listen more than I speak. I include affected and interested persons in the decision-making process. I expect, encourage, and celebrate different approaches from different administrators to the complex issues of the day. I read widely, and I reflect and review independently and with others. I think out loud a lot, and I try to ask the interesting questions. I act from information and from a sense of what is important. I trust people to mostly do the right thing, and I try to support them in that. I speak clearly and strongly for the needs of children and young people, and I attempt always to make decisions based on what's best for students.

Again, notice how the associate superintendent punctuated her set of beliefs with "I" messages as ""I believe," "I include," and "I act." No person can believe for another; therefore educators must develop their own statements of educational philosophy. Further, to be successful, administrators must act upon their beliefs.

Indeed, "Actions speak louder than words" is a familiar aphorism. Consider Christa Metzger (personal communication, February 21, 1992), a superintendent from California, who described how her belief in the ideals of public education led her to change the life of a student.

> I practice a strong belief in the ideals of public education for the survival of our democracy . . . . I will usually try to find a way for an individual to achieve his goals . . . . When I was principal of a K-8 school, I resisted all pressures by my staff to expel an eighth-grade girl who was having tremendous behavior problems in school. Her name was Mary, and she was always in trouble. Being raised by her grandmother, Mary had a very disturbed home life. She probably spent more time in my office than in her classes. But I never gave up on Mary, in spite of the teachers' desire to "kick her out." The results of my efforts were rewarded in a fantastic way. Approximately six years after Mary had left the eighth grade I received a phone call from her on Thanksgiving evening telling me that she had gotten married and that she was naming her first child after me. I had not heard anything from Mary during all those years and did not hear anything else from her for approximately the next ten years. One day I received a letter from the child whom she had named after me wanting to establish contact with her "Aunt" Christa. This child, who is now 11 years old, and I correspond on a regular basis, and I believe this relationship will have positive consequences for her in the future. In conclusion I agree that success is based on a complex set of factors. In my own case, I would attribute it to hard work and determination, a desire always to grow and learn from every experience, a degree of native intelligence and developed ability to analyze situations and solve problems, an action orientation (I don't just talk about things that need to be done—I organize the resources to get the job done), a willingness to accept and in fact encourage others to give critical feedback, a basic belief in the goodness of people, and some luck to have been able to "see opportunities," that is to be in the right place at the right time. Last, I want to credit many others who recognized talents or skills I might have had and helped me to develop them.

How school administrators can make a difference in the lives of students was also related by Patricia Popple (personal communication, February 6, 1993), an elementary principal from Wisconsin.

> I actively work on individual cases where I know I can make a difference. For example, the first school day a little girl walked into our mentally

retarded class, I knew she was not retarded. I vocalized that; I insisted she be mainstreamed into the kindergarten room so she could be with others because she said absolutely nothing; I told our needs assessment team that I didn't think she belonged there. I repeated my message to the special education department and to the psychologist, the social worker, the foster mother, and so on. The child could not be accurately assessed because she was delayed in language development. The teacher tried to teach the child to sign, but I insisted this was not appropriate in that few people in general life know sign language and that this child would have to learn some speech in that she could vocalize some. This past year she was fully mainstreamed. You cannot imagine my delight when we discovered she was able, in her own way, to read second-grade reading material and correctly answer questions about the material read. Several more staff members began to understand what I was saying and more people began to see the child in a different way. She blossomed this year . . . . The excellent work of my teaching staff and our work as a team will, we hope, make life different for this child.

ACADEMICS

Many topics can fit under the heading "Academics." One danger of using this heading is that the goal of schooling can be too narrowly construed and limited to intellectual development, the acquisition of abstract knowledge, and book learning. Because members of society have such broad expectations of education, clarifying the purpose of schooling becomes essential.

Mission

The leadership of superintendents is vital in clarifying the mission of a district, as a superintendent from Georgia noted. "The most important contribution any school superintendent can make is to understand thoroughly his school system, its mission, its philosophy, its objectives, and its learning climate. The ultimate goal is to offer all children the educational opportunities they need to be successful in a changing world."

An assistant superintendent from Pennsylvania linked his success with establishing a mission statement that clearly points the way for further action.

I believe the primary reason for my success in an administrative role is my possession of a philosophy that requires establishment of a mission statement and delineation of objectives in any responsibility undertaken. Persons involved appreciate understanding the reason for the activity and what will materialize from their efforts. Such indications also allow persons to focus on the task and begin to formulate long-range plans that will operate in accordance with the decisions. I have found that involving others serves to motivate individuals to become more involved, thus allowing participants to assume ownership.

A high school principal from Alabama provided an anecdote that revealed how the concept of mission can permeate a school and lead to recognition of its importance.

> For the past eight years, I have begun each year at our first faculty meeting talking about goal setting individually and organizationally—often to looks of "What in the world is he talking about now—not goals again, I hope!" But I have persisted, and with a little help from a local textile corporation, I think we have turned the corner with folks believing there is really something to this craziness of mine. Two years ago, during the summer, I brought a diverse group of people together to develop a mission statement for our school. After two days of intense discussion we agreed on our mission statement. Then next, I had to sell it to the faculty—a much more difficult task, and one that is really ongoing. My next task was to require academic departments to develop mission statements, and our final task will be to analyze each course we teach based on these mission statements to help determine our effectiveness. That textile corporation has its corporate headquarters in our community. One of my teachers whose husband works for the corporation approached me one day to say she had a sweatshirt for me that she thought I would really enjoy. The shirt was a sample made up for a potential buyer. Her husband had brought it home for her to work out in. Little did he know that I would be working out in it. The front of that shirt was emblazoned with the purchasing company's mission statement and on the back were its operating values! As the teacher handed me the shirt, she said, "Looks like you weren't so crazy after all."

A personal mission drives a superintendent from Arkansas. He believes in what he does and obtains rewards from pursuing that mission. His mission compels him to find ways to improve educational opportunities for students and their achievement.

> I believe in what I do. To lead a team of educators in the teaching of all children under our supervision is an immense challenge. The needs are great. There is so much to do. I can think of no greater mission, and when we are successful I can think of no greater reward. I am enthralled with the potential of a number of restructuring initiatives. Those strategies that better engage the passive learners should be a major focus. Specifically cooperative learning, interdisciplinary teaching, writing across the curriculum, and "student as worker" are paying dividends in student

achievement. Further, to give emphasis to the creation of a "thinking classroom" will be a major theme for the approaching school year.

The mission of the importance of public education has energized Donna W. Saiki (personal communication, July 22, 1991), a high school principal from Hawaii. She has sought to optimize educational opportunities and to maintain an optimistic attitude about those around her.

Having a strong sense of mission about the importance of public education is perhaps at the core of my being. Inherent in this mission is the quest to optimize educational opportunities for all students. To do this I feel compelled to know my students and school thoroughly, to interact with as many members of the school community as I can, and to attend all school functions . . . . Lastly, I firmly believe that in life you will find whatever it is you look for. I always look for the positive and best in people and situations and have always been surrounded by wonderful students and teachers.

Academic Excellence

Decades ago, Gardner (1961) raised critical questions about excellence in education. The search for excellence has not diminished in time, nor is it limited to educators for excellence is also the rallying cry for leaders in business, industry, and other public and private sector enterprises. Excellence may be unreachable, yet unless educators pursue excellence they will neither approach it nor approximate much of a semblance of it.

For a high school principal from North Dakota, the search for excellence undergirded his philosophy of education. He expanded his dedication to academic excellence toward other deeply held beliefs about students, teachers, and community service.

As a school administrator, I am totally dedicated to academic excellence in education. I feel strongly that all students can learn and that the sole reason for a school to exist is to give students the best education possible . . . . It is my belief that teachers are the core of a good education, and I constantly try to improve morale, keep teachers abreast of current educational trends, allow the staff to travel and attend workshops, seminars, and so on, evaluate and supervise them as often as possible, and make a conscientious effort to act immediately upon any requests I receive from teachers . . . . It is important for me to be involved in the community, and I presently serve on the executive board for the chamber of commerce, am involved in church and other service-minded organizations.

Notice how another high school principal, one from Pennsylvania, organized his thoughts about excellence, professionalism, supporting staff and students, learning, and innovation.

1. Maintain strong commitment to excellence and to professionalism:
   a. Have high expectations for yourself and those who work with/for you.
   b. Model the behaviors you espouse.
   d. Do it right!
   e. Develop a strong work ethic.
2. Be supportive of the staff and students:
   a. Be a good listener (open door) and communicator.
   b. Know your staff, students, and community.
   c. Involve staff, students, parents, and community members in the decision making.
3. Be a learner and an innovator:
   a. Develop a knowledge base for what you are doing.
   b. Be a risk taker and change agent.

William J. Pappas (personal communication, January 21, 1992), a high school principal from Michigan, linked academic achievement with the concept of equity.

While everyone outside is complaining about academic achievement, we maintain very high academic achievement. We still recognize the need for all the other programs for our students, and that speaks to the equity issue . . . . Equity within the school means the opportunity of access to all kids to everything within the school. It's not just a matter that classes and activities and athletics are available, but it means that all programs are available to kids.

Wanda Gunn (personal communication, March 16, 1992), a director of curriculum in Louisiana, provided a worthwhile reminder that no compromises should be made on excellence. The charge of a "rising tide in mediocrity" in education, as trumpeted in *A Nation at Risk*, can and should be resisted by administrators in their pursuit of excellence.

I believe in fairness for all those working within my supervision. Just as favoritism had no place in my classroom as a teacher, it has no place in my administrative working environment. I believe strongly that people do become what is expected of them. There is no place for procrastination in a successful administrative role. I believe that tasks, no matter how insignificant they might seem, should be completed on time and correctly. I believe that a compromise on excellence is a compromise on character, whether as an individual or as an entire school system. When we accept

mediocrity in education, we accept mediocrity as human beings. I believe
that excellence should be the goal for all local, state, and national education.

Borders and Boundaries

Where do the boundaries of academics lie? An interesting perspective was
provided by a superintendent from Oklahoma whose sense of responsibility
extended far beyond his school district's borders. Notice he first referred to working
"for and with others in the field of education" and not to one or more sites of
employment. His belief has compelled him to act as an advocate of quality education
for children, unlimited by geography and attendance borders.

I have attained some success in education as a result of having the ability
to work for and with others in the field of education. I feel school
administrators must take into account the importance of education for all
children regardless of where the children reside. We sometimes become
so concerned with the students in our own districts that we lose concern
for those outside our district. As an elected leader of our state administrators
association, I have attempted to be an advocate of quality education for
children regardless of their residence.

Instructional Autonomy

A high school principal from New York contended that teachers must have
instructional autonomy. What are your reactions to the ideas in the following
statement? What kinds of group dynamics might you expect to find in this principal's
school?

I believe it is crucial that teachers own their curriculum and that they
possess significant instructional autonomy. Assuming (and an
administrator must) competence and a sound knowledge base, instruction
becomes an investigative exercise in group dynamics. I enjoy participating
with teachers and students in this exercise.

Smith (1994) reported six norms for facilitating high commitment on the part
of staff members: (1) screen incoming staff, (2) invest in teacher knowledge and
authority, (3) encourage new ideas and risk taking, (4) distribute duties and
leadership across the organization, (5) humanize the work environment, and
(6) focus on performance, not compliance. For the second norm, she described
how instructional autonomy exists in one high school.

Invest in Teacher Knowledge and Authority. Once hired, talented
individuals are not left to languish. When high commitment is present,

investment can be made up front. Teachers are not obliged to prove themselves before controlling their work or getting things they need. Both individually and departmentally, Westside teachers enjoy very high levels of freedom and autonomy, which it is assumed they will use productively. (Smith, 1994, 45)

Quality Education

To what extent can a person in a position of authority, such as a superintendent of schools, become "an advocate of quality education for children" without the support and efforts of teachers? The beliefs of a middle school principal from Georgia about students and their primacy focused her role upon instructional leadership. Notice how she concluded her remarks. Would that all educational administrators loved their jobs!

I am a child advocate and my focus is on what is best for students. To achieve this focus, our school exudes a very positive, inviting climate to all. I believe that all students can learn and to that end, I maintain and communicate high expectations to staff and students. As the instructional leader in my school, it is my responsibility to promote and to protect instructional activities and instructional time. Above all else, I am a teacher who is also a leader. I care about my staff and students and I let them know it. I try to model what I expect of others. I love what I do!

Beliefs in the importance of education, the need for quality education for children, instructional autonomy for teachers to provide a quality education, and instructional leadership fit well with the remarks of an elementary school principal from Louisiana: "School improvement is not an event—it is a process. It is a never-ending process because there is and should always be room for improvement. My philosophy could most clearly be defined as 'If you can dream it, you can do it.'" Her dream of school improvement, a never-ending process, is a fitting capstone to the importance of academics to school administrators.

LEARNERS

Respondents to Project Success had definite ideas about one set of their customers—learners, or "kids," as they were often called. When outstanding administrators spoke of learners, they spoke of them with fondness, respect, and warmth and often indicated that the success, enjoyment, and satisfaction they enjoyed often came from working directly with students.

Kids First

What should be the number one priority of school administrators? The respondents to Project Success emphasized that the needs of students, or "kids," come first as illustrated in this remark by a middle school principal from Wisconsin. He also noted the necessity of working with staff and the home.

> As an administrators you must realize you are dealing with people in a business where "kids come first." One must have or develop the attitude and philosophy that allows you to deal with staff on a shared decision basis. An inservice program is essential to prepare staff for those responsibilities and expectations. Major in these responsibilities are the expectations for home/school contacts.

Percy Clark (personal communication, January 14, 1992), a superintendent from Indiana, noted his belief in the relationship between effective schools and their primary purpose. Regardless of the demands placed upon administrators, Clark contended, one question must be answered: Is this decision in the best interest of kids?

> My basic belief is that effective schools know that "schools exist for kids"; in other words, effective schools and effective school systems never forget their primary purpose and mission. Schools are expected to meet the countless demands of their communities on a daily basis, and sometimes these demands are overwhelming, causing the school district to lose sight of its primary purpose. Effective school districts do not allow their priorities to be confused . . . as they make their decisions about meeting various demands . . . and it is my duty and obligation to maintain a proper perspective by keeping this responsibility before us. Whenever I have a difficult decision to make regarding the direction of our school district, I always ask myself, "Is this in the best interest of our kids?"

The philosophy in a junior high school in Missouri incorporates several factors related to the concept that all kids can learn. Not all students can learn at the same rate, but they can learn when outcomes are stated clearly and when supportive features such as a positive school climate and inservice training are present.

> Our school philosophy is outcome based. We have worked with teachers over the last four years and now operate this way schoolwide. (1) We believe that success breeds success. (2) All kids can learn, but not at the same time; thus we have to expand the opportunity to learn. (3) Students learn better when the wanted outcomes are clear to all concerned. (4) Have high expectations for all the kids and provide such a climate in the classrooms throughout the school. (5) Provide the inservice [training] necessary to make it happen and lead the way.

Putting the needs of students first prompted Fred Anderson (personal communication, October 14, 1991), a high school principal from Montana, to set a balance among many kinds of educational opportunities, from school activities to scholastic endeavors.

> I believe I am an outstanding school administrator because I put the needs of all my students first. Successful administrators must always strive to maintain balance so that all students receive the optimum educational opportunities regardless of their station in the educational process. This balance projects beyond scholastic considerations encompassing all school activities. I believe the concept described by this statement is important enough that I consider it a key component in my educational philosophy. I believe balance must be initiated at the very roots of the curriculum process . . . . One of my key responsibilities as instructional leader is to ensure that every student receives the optimum educational opportunities, without regard to his or her personal background or the course of study he or she is pursuing . . . . It is essential that the accomplishments of the speech/drama team, language clubs, vocational education student organizations, or any other student group receive as much recognition and encouragement as does the state championship basketball team. Special efforts must be made to ensure that each of the organizations realizes that it is very important to the welfare of our school. This can be reflected in many ways, however; one is by providing equal weight on scholarship review committees, student recognition programs, and so on, for active involvement in any organization or activity that is part of the school. The balance concept also has to be handled delicately but firmly, between activities and scholastic endeavors . . . . Perhaps what it boils down to is striving to make certain that every student, whether he or she has been in an accelerated program or receiving special services be given the opportunity to increase his or her self-worth, to experience success, both scholastically and in activities, and through that success to build confidence both as a person and as a student.

Doug Cobb (personal communication, December 31, 1991), a superintendent from Wyoming, added other dimensions that result from putting students first. In his view, everything must be done to enhance the education of students and to contribute to their success.

> The students must come first in any school district. We are here for the successful learning of all students . . . . I believe in democratic leadership and participatory management. I also believe that I should serve as a model for the rest of the staff in the district. I believe in professional growth for myself as well as others. I try to keep abreast of the latest innovations and trends in education and take those that I feel best meet the needs of the school district and put them into my vision and attempt to adopt or adapt

it if I feel it will enhance the education of our students and make them more successful.

A refreshing view about students was provided by an elementary school principal from Oklahoma: "People send you the best kids they have—if they had any more they'd send them too, and they want them back better than they were when you got them."

An administrator in Utah projected a comprehensive view of education from his personal perspective.

> First, I wanted to teach school because I love children and I think that attending school can help them to lead happy and successful lives. I still feel that everything done in our schools should be done because it is good for our children—for our students. I believe every child can learn and that parents, teachers, and administrators should work together to ensure that each child does learn . . . . Second, I believe service is what public education is all about; that when we commit our resources and energies to do the best we can for students, everyone benefits. Excellence really can be a state of mind, and many benefits can result from positive thinking. Basically, I enjoy helping people—including children—feel good about themselves.

All Children Can Learn

Two school administrators, a junior high school principal from West Virginia and a high school principal from Kansas, respectively, affirmed a belief that is commonly found among educators—that all children can learn.

> I truly believe that all children can learn and that when they don't, we as educators have failed.
>
> Our focus is on student learning. We strongly believe and practice the belief that all children can learn. We expect our teachers to be teachers of students first, and subject matter teachers second. We expect our students to take on their responsibilities in the learning process and for all students to take the minimum academic subjects needed to assure them the option of attending a postsecondary program upon graduation. For example, we have eliminated all math classes below pre-algebra, which requires all students to complete Algebra I to graduate. Just as we believe that all children can learn, we also believe that all children can be taught the behavior necessary for a positive learning school climate and culture.

Another high school principal, one from Rhode Island, elaborated upon the principle that all students can learn. The belief that all students can learn leads to many behaviors that are predicated upon such a statement.

> *All* students can learn and schools exist to educate *all* students. Therefore, student learning must be the first priority of *all* the adults in our schools. Second, since much of the student learning that takes place in schools is influenced by teachers; teachers need to be the second priority of administrators. With these priorities in order, administrators need to remain current in educational research, trends, issues, and so on; to express trust and respect for students and teacher; to be accessible to both students and teachers; to spend time listening for both the overt and hidden messages of students and teachers; to provide opportunities, resources, and support for both students and teachers to be successful; to provide the motivation for students and teachers to allow them to improve and be creative in the teaching-learning process; to give students and teachers the authority to implement their ideas to improve learning and receive the rewards for their achievement; and to be prepared to support and defend their basic philosophical principles and priorities in all arenas and to all audiences.

Compare the preceding statement with that of Jimmy Johnson (personal communication, October 15, 1991), a high school principal from South Carolina, who also affirmed that every child can and will learn if teachers and administrators provide the inspiration for learning.

> We believe that every child can learn and will learn if given the appropriate inspiration. It's our job as teachers and administrators (who must team together) to discover the appropriate inspiration for our students. My job is to be the master teacher, one who can teach effectively as well as assist others in whatever ways necessary for them to be effective as well. We try to make our school an inviting place to come to (attractive, clean, safe, with a caring atmosphere). We try to ensure that we have a good time as best we can (while maintaining order/discipline in its proper perspective). Finally, we try to be as flexible and open to change as possible, giving all our publics (students, teachers, parents, community members) the opportunity to make decisions that will make our school a better place for teachers to teach and for students to learn.

A book by Charles Murray and Richard Herrnstein, *The Bell Curve*, may cause educators to rethink what they believe about "all children can learn." Not that their belief should be changed, but that the relationship of intelligence to learning may be challenged from different perspectives. Murray and Herrnstein have raised public consciousness about numerous issues as they contend that social policy must be overhauled to account for this: Welfare, education and affirmative action programs aimed at helping the poor should be scrapped because the recipients have limited intelligence and cannot benefit from a helping government hand. Others, of course, have made the case that the limitations of poor persons are the very reason that they need assistance to make sure they are productive citizens. (Why IQ Isn't Destiny, 73)

A debate sparked by *The Bell Curve* may be more than philosophical in nature, for it may trigger untold reactions about allocation of resources for children— from the brightest children to those with learning difficulties.

The concepts "all children can learn" and "kids come first" have bearing upon many features of schooling. Educators who espouse such concepts about students should attach great importance to what is in the curriculum, how the curriculum is delivered, how well the curriculum is developed, and how well learning is appraised. Educators have devoted sporadic attention to the latter, for example, and have long supported the measurement of student learning through standardized testing programs—at least as long as test results are good. Alternative forms of student learning are increasingly advocated as better means of measuring student learning. "Authentic assessment" is proposed to be an advanced form of measuring student learning because it is a method in which many kinds of evidence are collected to document what students have learned. Attention should be directed to forming a framework that links learning objectives, instructional practices, and assessment methods so that the teaching-learning process is viewed as a whole (Wraga, 1994) and extends beyond lip service to popular ideas.

Learning Styles

Administrators who believe that all children can learn have added some corollaries, conditions for learning, and supportive factors to their belief. A junior high school principal from Missouri noted her belief in the functionality of learning styles.

I'm a major believer in the theory of learning styles and I've tried to direct my staff in their own knowledge base in this area. I've gone through the process of assessing the teaching styles and learning styles of my staff. As I work with them on various issues of improvement or improvement for the school, I try to accommodate their learning styles in our staff development sessions and faculty meetings and in general work with them, whether they are auditory, visual, tactile, or kinesthetic. I try to model for teachers what I want them to do for kids in the classroom.

Child Advocate

One role of a school administrator is to be an advocate for children. An elementary principal from Wisconsin described how such a view of his role permeated his job description and actions, his very being, resulting in benefits for children of his district.

Being an advocate for children begins with my job description, where being an advocate is a written part of my role as building principal . . . . In these times educational leaders must be willing to speak out despite the obvious risks. That means that we may not be the most popular people with some individuals, but it is a risk worth taking. For example, several years ago the board of education, under pressure from a segment of the taxpayers, felt the need to reduce programs and/or increase class size to effect a reduction in taxes. As educational leaders, the school administrators argued against such acts, citing the impact it would have on kids. It certainly was not the popular thing to do with some board members, and we were somewhat chastised by them for our vocal stand. The end result was that programs were not cut and we maintained the class size philosophy we had worked to set. There were some cuts in the areas of supplies and equipment, and we are still attempting to catch up in those areas as a result.

Carole Kennedy (personal communication, December 31, 1991), an elementary school principal in Missouri, explained why school administrators should be advocates of children.

I believe that educators are at times guilty of falling into the same pattern as parents. In our quest to have orderly classrooms where learning can happen, we insist on obedience to *our* set of rules, rules that are imposed on children with no input from them and thus little understanding on their part of why rules should be followed. Little time is spent teaching kids what is inappropriate. In reality, many times what is accepted as appropriate at home is in direct conflict with expected behavior at school. An example: Some kids are told to fight when things don't go as they want; schools punish for fighting. Teachers and principals seem bent on schoolwide discipline plans that treat each child exactly the same and may include out-of-school suspension. I believe that to treat all children the same is a great injustice—they are not alike and deserve to be dealt with as individuals. Rather than be suspended, students need to be in school and taught to solve problems. Dignity is a very personal, very important part of an individual. When dignity is taken away, an essential element of self-worth is gone. Children begin to believe that they are bad, unworthy of receiving love, unable to learn, so they quit trying. Children then become what they think we think they are.

Developmental Needs

Educators know much about how children, adolescents, and adults learn. Their beliefs translate into many features of schooling, from daily schedules to classroom design to instructional strategies. The developmental needs of students vary in many ways, but educators must provide means of accommodating large numbers of students to provide efficient instruction. A middle school principal from Missouri identified several features of his school's program to meet the needs of a particular age group.

> I strongly believe that middle schools must be tailored to meet the special needs of the preadolescent, and my building's program includes team teaching, cooperative learning, exploratory offerings, an advisement program, and a strong program for student recognition . . . . My district believes in parent and staff involvement in decision making, and I have a seventeen-member team comprised of administrators, teachers, parents, and community business members. This team will make decisions in the areas of curriculum and instruction.

ADMINISTRATION

Administrators have definite convictions about fundamental beliefs, public education, instructional leadership, and the primacy of learners. They also have decided opinions about how to administer schools and what administrative and organizational factors lead to success.

Climate

Experienced administrators can walk into a school and sense the climate of the building within a few minutes. A climate within an organization is built over time and is composed of countless factors and conditions. Successful administrators do not let a climate develop or exist without direction but assume a responsibility for creating a climate that is supportive of people, programs, and improvement. Mark A. Mitrovich (personal communication, April 27, 1992), an assistant superintendent from the state of Washington, affirms the value of creating a climate that fosters growth.

> I believe that by creating a climate that encourages risk taking, supports success, and recognizes setbacks as true learning experiences, we reduce significantly the fear of change. Rather than back away from challenges, we meet them with an attitude that sees them as open doors for growth. My part in this process is fostering that climate while providing the instructional leadership that gives a sense of vision to our total endeavor.

A former superintendent from Kentucky linked two factors, work ethic and organizational climate, as crucial to success. The creation of a supportive climate does require effort in planning, working with people, pushing for goals, and establishing conditions that foster a desired organizational climate.

> My philosophy for success includes an incredible work ethic that is the result of being part of a family where hard work was always the first expectation. In addition, I believe the success of any organization is the strength of the people involved—the implementors—be they custodians, central office staff, teachers, food service staff, or bus drivers. My goal has always been to develop an organizational climate where such a shared vision and responsibility can be nurtured and grow. This requires being open and available.

A principal from New Hampshire echoed the preceding comments and added other dimensions, such as individuality, encouragement of divergent ideas, and the concept of family within a school.

> I believe that I am an outstanding school administrator because of my commitment to a set of ideals that focus on education as a lifelong process. I feel strongly that every person is unique in his or her ability, learning style, and personality. My responsibility as a school administrator is to create, foster, and maintain a school climate where all dimensions of individuality are recognized, honored, and respected. By modeling those aspects of leadership I feel are important to success—hard work, positive value system, visibility, dedication, and high work ethic—I set the tone and pace for student and adult growth in our school. I am actively involved in all aspects of our school programs and strive to encourage risk taking in decision making. Creating an atmosphere where divergent ideas are encouraged and respected is a dimension of leadership that I feel makes me an outstanding administrator. Finally, most important to me is the strong sense of family that exists in our school . . . . I feel strongly that an outstanding administrator is one who constantly strives to create and maintain such an atmosphere.

The importance of providing cultural leadership was proposed by a director of instructional management and curriculum from Colorado.

> If I were to ascribe my success as a school administrator to any one component, it would have to be that of understanding the critical importance of cultural leadership in creating schools that make a difference. While skills in management and administration are certainly necessary as well, I don't see them as the "special ingredient" that makes one a really effective leader . . . . From my perspective, clear values and purpose are the core element of cultural leadership, and the other factors often discussed

are how you infuse the culture of a school with those values and that sense of purpose. I have a very strong value system regarding education and the way all the people involved in the system should treat one another. I also have a very strong belief about the purposes of education, which is to educate all children and educate them well. I tried to model these values and beliefs in almost every aspect of what I did as an administrator. I believe outstanding leaders in any field are articulate about their profession and are able to create bridges between theory and practice. This means that a successful leader/cultural leader must remain extremely well informed about education and the political, psychological, and pedagogical developments in the field. I have made a strong effort to remain very current in my reading and to be able to share practical implications of that reading with colleagues and staff. I believe this articulated knowledge base provided me with credibility when I "pushed and pulled" people into unknown territory.

What happens when value statements become part of a school district's culture? A superintendent from Oregon, Alfred H. Meunier (personal communication, February 5, 1992), related an incident that hinged upon the visibility and acceptance of value statements that his district had adopted.

What I feel a need to emphasize is that the value statements, if worthwhile, must become a part of the culture of a district. Once this happens, they infuse our daily behavior with staff, students, parents, and the public. The key is having the leadership behave in ways that let others know that they "walk their talk" when it comes to value statements . . . . We were working with the staff development committee and the usual barriers of staff time and financial resources became the issue. After about twenty minutes a teacher pointed to the value statement that indicates a belief in "developing-fostering an attitude of self-renewal." He said, "Either we believe in this or we don't. It is just that simple." Within fifteen minutes the teachers found time and the district found money. Value statements are that simple. They either become part of the culture and ethos or they don't become part of the culture and ethos.

A high school principal from Utah described how he carried out his belief in the principal's role in creating a positive climate in a school.

I have been a firm believer in the climate of a school and believe a principal can have a real impact in creating the climate. To that extent, we decided to adorn the walls with beautiful art prints that we purchased from art galleries from anywhere from $3 to $10 each. Community volunteers framed them, and we now have on all three floors a beautiful art gallery of prints of the most famous paintings in the world. We had heard a lot about the powers of heavy-metal music. Thus, we instituted a program to play classical music over the public address system in the hallways. We have found a definite mellowing but upbeat effect in study and in the arts. We now oft-times get requests from students that come in and say things like, "Would you play some Paganini?" We find it very refreshing to know that once students hear classical music, they develop an appreciation for it.

Changes in climate can be accomplished in several ways. Consider the approach of Gerald McCoy (personal communication, February 5, 1992), a superintendent from Minnesota. He described the results of efforts in gender equity.

When I became superintendent, my first commitment was to equalize the male and female administrative ratio. Once that was accomplished, new worlds and wonderful possibilities opened to us all. Equalizing the gender ratio increased our sensitivity on a number of issues and gave the distaff side a chance to influence the practices and policies of the district. In effect, the pawns became players. An unexpected benefit was the increased civility in our administrative meetings. We became wide-eyed empathic listeners, anxious to shed the image of sexism. We learned that our actions needed to change if we were going to create a partnership where the dignity and worth of each individual was respected. We discussed openly what constitutes harassment, sexism, and ignorance on the part of both women and men. Any anger or resentments has washed away with dialogue and time. The result of equalizing the administrative ratio cannot be fully measured, but early on, the trust level in the school system began to improve. Risk taking increased and words like "team" and "partnership" became common as we developed strategies to create a learning environment where all students could be successful.

Collaboration

Successful administrators know they have sole responsibility for some functions and duties that only they are to perform. In the creation of a positive climate, successful administrators also know they cannot be absolute despots. They cannot run things only their way, as pointed out by a high school principal from Indiana.

[I have a] belief in the use of a collaborative style of management. I prefer to involve those who will be affected by decisions in making those decisions. Having been principal in two schools for a total of five years, I have been able to begin school improvement programs in both schools.

Compromise

The art of politics is reputedly based upon compromise. Perhaps the art of school administration is also based upon compromise, for few people can always get their way. Roy D. Nichols (personal communication, March 22, 1992), a superintendent from Georgia, subscribed to making reasonable compromises.

> I believe in reasonable compromise and have accepted the fact that often a half loaf is better than none. At the same time, I realize that a crumb is just that—it can be seen but it has very little substance. Therefore, like all decision makers, I must often make a judgment as to whether a compromise position is worth pursuing. If it isn't, I am willing to admit that we have reached a point upon which we can agree to disagree. I also believe that for most disagreements, an acceptable solution can be found providing enough energy is put into the search for this solution, the people involved truly want to find a solution, and enough time passes to allow people to see the problem for what it is without the fog of pride standing between them and reason. I don't have a power fixation, and I am willing to gracefully back away from a proposal for the good of the school system.

Serving Customers

Much of the writing on innovation and quality focus upon the concept of meeting customers' needs. Successful school administrators recognize the need to satisfy their customers, as Ruth Handley (personal communication, May 31, 1992), a superintendent in Florida, reiterated.

> I think many young and narrowly experienced school leaders fear (and thus resist) inviting parents, businesspersons, and "mere" taxpayers into the design and management of public schools. But we are going to *have* to open these doors if public education is going to survive . . . and we *should*. The students and the general public are our customers. We must learn to serve their needs. Pedagogy cannot exist in a vacuum. Society demands more and more services from the public schools in more and more aspects of life. We cannot address all the issues through traditional instructional processes. We must have the input from others. And we must accept their input in a spirit of genuine appreciation. This includes learning to understand and value the diversities that mark our nation.

Decision Making

Shared decision making, participative management, and similar terms are embraced by administrators such as Florence B. Morton (personal communication, March 6, 1992), a high school principal from Kentucky.

I believe in and have included in my administrative behavior the contributions of parents, and business and political authorities, as well as teachers and other school personnel. Regardless of my style and my philosophy of education, I do not expect that all my teachers and staff members will always agree with me. I know that any decision I may make may be approved by one group and at the same instant meet with opposition from another group. When I say that I and potent social forces outside the school must be facilitators, I refer specifically to the need of support from parents, business leaders, and community leaders and their understanding of the aims, purposes, and objectives of American education. Certainly their influences in different sectors of the community are most valuable in communicating the intent of the school.

An elementary school principal from Utah supported decision making at the level of implementation.

I believe that when adequate authority and/or leadership is given at the school level, many important decisions affecting scheduling, personnel, curriculum, and the use of resources will be made by the people who are in the best position to make them, those that are most aware of the problems and needs. Only by meaningfully involving educators in their own professional destiny, by involving parents who are stakeholders, as well as students who are the recipients of our efforts, will real concern, creativity, and initiative be stimulated.

Interpersonal Relations

If decision making can be accepted as the nature of administration, then perhaps a corollary is that decisions are made about, with, and through people. The effect of good decision making is not limited to the authority of an administrator to make decisions but is much affected by how others perceive administrators' actions regarding decisions. A former school administrator from Colorado stressed the importance of effective interpersonal relationships.

Leaders must be able to build effective interpersonal relationships with all people, relationships characterized by fairness, openness, honesty, and trust. The key things that I do, because I believe they are important are these: (1) I honor people and demonstrate respect for who they are and where they have been in their life. (2) I take time for people by showing an interest in them and listening to them. (3) I always make a concerted effort to do what I say I will do and follow through. This creates predictability and builds trust, even if the person disagrees with me. (4) I share personal stories and aspects of my life in professional relationships, which demonstrates vulnerability and humanness and reduces power inherent in formal roles and positions in organizations. (5) I always try to make sure that a person never "loses face" when dealing with sensitive personnel/human issues. I always try to keep in mind how I would want to be treated and to take the extent possible to react that way. (6) I value diversity and the richness that diverse culture, ideology, political thought, and perspective bring to organizations and communities. I honor people and show respect for them as human beings regardless of their culture, socioeconomic status, or gender. People, no matter what their position in life or where they came from, want to feel they are valuable and respected. I've been able to demonstrate my value of diversity and build effective relationships with people who are very different from me because I hold this as a strong value. One other thing that I believe has helped me to succeed in leadership roles has been my continued belief in lifelong learning. I continue to read, take classes, attend workshops, and put myself in situations and learning experiences that stretch me because they push me outside of my comfort zone and cause me to grow. As readily as our society (world) and information bases are changing, I know that as soon I feel comfortable and start to seek comfort at the expense of embracing new thought and ways of doing things that stretch me, I will have then begun the journey to ineffectiveness.

Leadership

Doug Christensen (personal communication, January 24, 1992), associate commissioner of the Nebraska Department of Education, provided insight into the kind of leadership that school administrators need to furnish.

It is important that leaders make sure the right questions are being asked so that "right answers" can be found. Many times in the restructuring of organizations we continue to ask the same old questions and as a result get the same old answers. It is more important to make sure we are asking the right questions, which often means asking new questions that have not been asked before. For example, in reforming schools it is not the question, "How should we restructure our schools?" It is, "What should we be restructuring about education?" Sometimes it is asking questions in the right order. The questions that should be driving leadership in education reform today are (1) What should students learn? (2) How do they best learn it? The corollary to "live the questions" is "the answer is in the struggle."

Cheryl Pongratz (personal communication, February 8, 1992), a middle school principal from New Mexico, examined leadership from the standpoint of style. Her reflections upon her leadership style may give pause for similar reflection.

When I decided to go into school administration, several courses I took had, as part of the content, various instruments to evaluate personal/ leadership style. I perceived myself as fairly authoritarian. In retrospect, I am amused at that because in thirteen years as a teacher and the same number as a parent I was far from authoritarian. Rather than authoritarian, I found that the same principle that governed other aspects of my life also governed my leadership style: belief in the ability of people to make good decisions, belief that there is not "one right way" to do things, belief that people who have sufficient information do not necessarily act totally in self-interest but will act for the greater good, and other Pollyanna-type beliefs like that. For me, a significant key for getting people involved was the issue of information. The staff had been used to being in the dark and being told what was happening after the fact. Even today, after eleven years of working with some of these folks, I often get comments that they appreciate the information sharing (their memories are long of how it used to be). We must be open with information not only with staff but with students.

In Connecticut, a junior high school principal developed a program designed to develop leadership among his faculty members.

An innovative education program that I implemented enables skilled teachers who believe they might have an interest in educational administration to obtain first-hand experiences with administrative tasks. As a result of the practical knowledge and experiences they obtain in the program, administrative aspirants are able to reach a valid decision as to whether they possess the requisite skills to function as an educational leader. Approximately twenty educators have been involved in our administrative aspirant program, and twelve of them are now in positions of educational leadership. Each of them feels strongly that the experiences gained through the program were a vital factor in their successful candidacy for a leadership position. Although the majority of those who have obtained leadership positions have not stayed in our district, we still believe the program has greatly benefited our community as well as the educational community beyond our district.

The Future

All administrators, at one time or another, struggle with how to peer into the future, find a light to travel by, or advance. One way to be proactive about future needs is to set goals, as Gerald Daley (personal communication, June 3, 1991), a superintendent from New Hampshire, advised.

I believe a successful school administrator must be more than a good manager. He or she must first and foremost be an educational leader. Educational leaders provide direction for their schools. They set goals and hold people accountable for reaching them. They have high expectations for both personnel and students. They care about people and they care about results.

Even after setting goals, accountability standards, and high expectations, administrators must engage in decision making. What better phrase more aptly describes the nature of administration than decision making? School administrators make hundreds of decisions each day. Gene Armstrong (personal communication, October 10, 1991), a high school principal from Nebraska, confirmed the basis for decision making and projected a reminder that decisions made today affect the future—the 21st century—soon to be upon us.

Decisions should be made keeping the welfare of students uppermost in our minds. If we can affirmatively answer the question, "Is it good for our students?" there is probably value in the decision .... Ownership for decision making should rest in large part with those most affected by that decision. The students we send out of our schools must be prepared for the 21st century by being able to handle change, even welcome it. Thus, we must be willing to look at ourselves to see that what we are providing our students allows them to be successful in their subsequent environment.

The imminence of the 21st century was also noted by John Bone (personal communication, November 25, 1991), an elementary school principal from Utah.

I believe that the development and implementation of exemplary programs require a level of site-based leadership that has foresight and vision. Often, instituting implementations that are based upon these characteristics places an educational leader in uncomfortable, often confronting situations. This is particularly true if this foresight is directed toward moving away from longstanding traditional practices. And yet a move away from traditional practices is inevitable if we are going to meet the needs of students as they interact within the 21st century.

The lessons of the past are likely to be repeated in the future. Some good lessons will be followed and some ignored. For example, responsible administrators do not set goals arbitrarily, capriciously, or without careful thought. An elementary school principal from North Carolina called to mind the value to be gained from research, substantive findings, sound reasoning, experience, and practice that together enable administrators to draw lessons from the past for projections into the future and to engage in reasoned risk taking.

> Another quality that has contributed to my success has been my willingness to "take a risk." I believe that it is very important to learn about new ideas and trends and give them a try. Effective schools philosophy is ingrained in me. I truly believe that if you continue to do as you have been doing, you will continue to get what you've been getting. Many times this is good. However, we must be willing to lead the way down new paths and have a vision of something better for our schools. Of course, visions and new ideas should be based on some type of research or intellectually sound reasoning.

A superintendent from Indiana, James Auter (personal communication, November 26, 1991), noted some important considerations that must be followed.

> We believe that schools can make a significant difference in the progress of our society. The stakes are very high and further change is required . . . . Our carefully developed educational philosophy should serve as our vision and guide as we participate in the improvement and restructuring process. Change will not come through coercion, nor command and control, but through carefully planned processes that develop collaboration and networking.

A superintendent from Louisiana saw the future encased in opportunities and administrators as agents to capitalize upon such opportunities.

> I have always tried to think in terms of what can be done as opposed to what can't be done. It is my belief that school administrators have to be change agents. They have to help others to understand the need for innovation, how to manage innovation, and how to accept the resulting change.

Bob Pellegrino (personal communication, April 16, 1992), a middle school principal from Wisconsin, shared his views on how his beliefs about mission, vision, change, shared decision making, and respect for students transformed attitudes about one major characteristic of middle schools.

> I believe I have a mission to share a vision with my students and staff that places an emphasis on the success of all students. Although I am often described as a change agent, I attempt to involve staff in a shared decision-making process whenever possible. I am aware that change occurs

over a period of time and needs the support and encouragement of the principal. I have found it of utmost importance to listen to what students have to say. This sounds like a simple truth, but I believe it is one we often forget. Listening doesn't necessarily mean I will always agree, but it demonstrates my respect for individuals. Our school initiated a teacher-advisee program two years ago. It has met with mixed reviews from both students and staff. A segment of each group has voiced a desire to see the program disbanded. I have met in small groups and individually with students to hear their concerns and identify possible solutions. The majority of students who wish to see the program abolished identified the lack of involvement and support by their advisor as their concern. They made a number of suggestions on how the program could be changed to improve it. I also met with staff to obtain the same input. The information I received from students was a critical factor in my ability to maintain the program for the upcoming school year. I strongly believe that the opportunity the teacher-advisee program offers to develop unique relationships between students and teachers is critical to the success of our school.

ATTRIBUTES AND CHARACTERISTICS

A superintendent of schools, now located in Minnesota, listed those attributes that contributed to his success.

I believe I possess the following attributes that contribute to my success:

- *Relationship with people.* Can relate to people, like to serve people, develop people, am sensitive to people's feelings and needs, am caring about people, and can lead or mobilize people to achievement.
- *Vision/Focus.* Can create a vision of the future, communicate it, and focus on plans and activities to move toward the vision created.
- *Substance/Integrity.* Am knowledgeable or have the curiosity and motivation to obtain new knowledge, have mission and purpose as an administrator, able to conceptualize, possess deep-seated beliefs and values about education and youth, possess the courage to practice what is believed and the integrity to gain and keep the trust of others.
- *Versatility/Creativeness.* Can relate to a variety of people, will take risks or be cautious as the situation demands, can understand the interrelatedness and connectedness of events, people, systems, purpose, and so on, to be creative, am flexible about ways to achieve results and possess the capacity to be patient, tolerant, cope with ambiguities yet demanding.
- *Performance/Confidence.* Have high expectations of self and others, work hard, mentally rehearse my performance ahead of time,

accomplish results, celebrate success, build confidence in others, am self-confident, enthusiastic, well organized, and assertive.

Les Anderson (personal communication, October 14, 1991), the principal of a middle school in North Dakota, also listed several characteristics.

There are certain commonalties that make for effective leaders in all fields of endeavor. I will list some of those characteristics and how they fit into my philosophy.

1. High expectations of self and others: I have very high expectations of myself and the people who are around me. I expect the best from myself and I expect the students and the staff to perform at a level they are capable of. I not only verbalize this philosophy but also model it every day of the school year. There are constant reminders around the school with the use of signs, displays, the marquee, assemblies, and PA announcement.
2. A values-driven work ethic: We work by the project and not by the hour.
3. Willingness to risk: We try to operate on the edge of our competence, which causes some setbacks, frustrations, and mistakes. We do not perceive these as failures but, rather, as learning experiences to help us to provide a better program.
4. Visionary: We set personal and professional goals for ourselves and the school. We have a vision and we know what we want to look like in five years. Our goals are clearly identified and in written form. We have a global perspective and we are mission driven.
5. Enthusiastic optimists: We think in terms of do's rather than in terms of do not. We look for ways to make things work instead of why it will not work.
6. Communicator: We treat the staff as professionals and expect them to act that way. We listen and provide accurate, honest assessment of situations.

Working with Others

Many administrators wrote about how successful administrators should approach working with others. A high school principal from Minnesota wrote about the respect that must be accorded others.

I believe all persons—each and everyone—have worth and dignity that differences of gender, race, culture, and physical, mental, and emotional characteristics do not make an individual more or less worthwhile. Thus,

I offer others respect, appreciation, and personal encouragement . . . . I consistently choose problem-solving approaches over conflict and power.

John Daggett (personal communication, February 6, 1992), a superintendent from Oregon, wrote:

First, I am a student of education. I believe I never know all the answers and I am constantly learning new things. Second, I base decisions on what I believe is in the best interest of the children we serve, Third, generally the people who work with me find the quality of their life is enhanced because I believe in the potential good of all people. Fourth, I believe in hiring the smartest, brightest people for a position. I am not intimidated by working with people who are more competent than me.

Harlan Else (personal communication, January 29, 1992), a superintendent from Colorado, tied two major belief statements together. "First of all, I believe every person has worth and is entitled to be treated with dignity and respect. Second, I believe that no matter how much I know, people must first trust me if I am going to have any success in facilitating the success of people in our organization."

A high school principal from Ohio, Dave McDaniel (personal communication, January 23, 1992), commented on the special relationship administrators have with their secretaries.

A successful principal has an outstanding secretary who can work in tandem as a partner in the job of administering the school. I believe this is paramount in the success of the building. A relationship of trust, admiration, respect, and confidentiality with the secretary must exist. There are few partners who have a successful operation where these characteristics are not obvious. The characteristics of talent, knowledge, quick thinking, and good judgment also have to be exhibited . . . . In many cases the principal's secretary has to make decisions, speak for the administrator, be the public relations outlet, and be the communicator in times of absence or unavailability of the building administrator. This trust relationship is absolute and must take place.

Perhaps the greatest joy of administrators is obtained from working with students. The adventure of helping students overcome obstacles was described by Cleveland Hammonds (personal communication, March 11, 1992).

Teaching and education is a great adventure. It is the task of administration to keep the adventure alive. Each child contains the potential to fulfill some need that society has. One example is a young high school sophomore who became pregnant. A member of the high school faculty told me that she felt that this student, if she could survive this crisis in her life, had a unique surprise. The teacher and others provided the young mother with the support and nurturing she needed to finish high school. The surprise was that she went from being an average student to becoming an honor student. She received a full scholarship at a prestigious private liberal arts college and plans to become a medical doctor. If I can ignite the fire of dedication, concern, and commitment in others, then I have performed my role as a leader. If you perform your role to find the most able, creative, determined, and dedicated professionals available, then you must, as a leader, provide freedom, support, and understanding so they can do their job.

Being Positive

The value of positive attitudes about the job, students, and community members was expressed by Richard Maas, a high school principal from Minnesota (personal communication, February 7, 1992).

I believe that you cannot be successful in any job unless you enjoy what you are doing. I look forward to coming to work each day. It is absolutely essential in this job to have an appreciation for the young people in our world and a desire for them to obtain the best educational experience. I enjoy working with students, and it is most rewarding to observe their growth and success. I also believe you must foster positive relations with parents and community members of the school district. Invitations to visit the school and participate in special programs allow them to feel they are a part of the educational process of the young people in their community.

Charles Edwards (personal communication, February 10, 1992), an elementary school principal from Kentucky, believes in the power of positive thinking and the power of positive actions as well. "I do not believe that anything happens by accident. Whatever happens, happens because a person, or a group of people, has willed it by creating the conditions under which it can and will happen. I believe in being positive about everything. If bad happens, how can I use it to our advantage?"

A high school principal from Missouri proposed a different way of viewing others by rephrasing an old adage. "I sincerely believe that people will reach the level of expectation set for them. As a leader, one must continue to extend those expectations. People also respond to trust and faith. I like the altered expression, 'If you give someone an inch, he or she will give you a mile.'"

An elementary principal from Oklahoma, Don Briix (personal communication, March 23, 1992), contrasted positive people with those with negative outlooks.

Outstanding administrators that I know seem to be positive people. They "reach out" to others and make them feel good, worthwhile, and important. People generally like people who make them feel good. Outstanding administrators have learned that this approach creates a nice work environment and high productivity in their school. Some administrators use the gloom and doom method. Everything is negative. There is never enough money for themselves or their school. The teachers are negative and at fault. The media is against education. The legislators are a bunch of crooks. The kids are a bunch of brats. The parents don't support the school. At first, some people may be agreeable to this person and fall into this same negative frame of mind. But sooner or later people begin to wonder about this administrator's leadership ability and question whether his heart is in the right place. They wonder about his ability to motivate and doubt that he has a vision and goals for his school. After a while, the people get tired of the negativism and the administrator is charged—"held accountable." He loses the respect of his staff, parents, students, and others. His ability to lead suffers, and people decide it is time for a change.

A middle school principal from Missouri noted how positive attitudes about people can permeate a school.

I believe that if a principal will spend all the time necessary to hire positive-thinking people that love children, feel proud to be in teaching, have a good sense of humor and a high energy level, that half of the success will be fulfilled. The other half of success comes from the principal who truly believes in the potential of his staff and maintains a supportive disposition of a full-fledged partner in the teaching-learning enterprise.

Another middle school principal, Gail Gates (personal communication, March 9, 1991) from Louisiana, described how her attitudes about people were evident in her administrative practices.

My philosophy has always been that as a school principal I manage people, not buildings. This is the premise upon which I work with my students, my staff, and the parents of my school's community. On a daily basis, I am sensitive to their ideas, concerns, and opinions. These are the people who constitute the degree of success a school is able to achieve. I include teachers in making decisions, encourage new ideas and experimentation, and trust teachers to take risks. I offer them support for taking the initiative in developing their own leadership skills. Our school community is a sharing place with much emphasis on cooperation and collegiality. Many teachers have told me at one time or another, "I didn't think I could accomplish that, but your encouragement and faith in me made me trust myself." My office door is always open to encourage communication and to share decision making.

Faith in people is basic to the success of an assistant superintendent from Washington.

The success I have had as an administrator stems from my faith in people. The challenge of encouraging others to be the best they can be is very rewarding to me. I believe people have unlimited potential. I like nurturing leadership qualities in others. I don't need to be in the limelight, but I do need to be respected by my colleagues. People are very important to me. I am dedicated to the education profession. I want to make an impact in the lives of kids. I want to see the conditions improve so all kids will be safe and successful.

A belief in human decency and self-worth was expressed by a middle school principal from Kansas.

I believe in human decency and self-worth. I respect each person as an individual; each with a unique gift to give. I don't have all the answers and I don't always know the best way to do things. I let my staff know that I welcome their input, knowledge, and expertise. This does leave me vulnerable at times, but I still work within a set of professional guidelines, boundaries, and/or limits. Those stretch and/or shrink accordingly, but they never disappear completely, so we don't get too far out in left field!

Patti Harrington (personal communication, April 8, 1992), an elementary principal from Utah, amplified how her respect for others translated into involving them in school operations.

"Involvement comes at the level of decision making," a wise mentor once told me. This is the underlying principle that has guided my leadership. I involve any person whom I then expect to delegate to regarding any work. Teachers help make instructional decisions, parents have direct input into the climate of the school and our community efforts, and support personnel are asked to advise me on matters related to their areas. Once involved, these people share and own the goal and then do their best work. My job, then, becomes one of delegation, high expectations, immense praise and support, and envisioning the next goal.

A superintendent from Michigan also noted the importance of involving others in reaching goals.

I believe much of my success has come from assigning responsibility and expecting accountability. As an administrator, I recognize the need to work through others to accomplish ends. Where I have had greatest success is in being able to align the goals of others with the goals that I, as an administrator, have been seeking. Critical to this process is the willingness and the self-confidence to delegate commensurate responsibility and authority to the person performing the task and to be a good listener.

Setting High Expectations

The line between success and failure was described by a superintendent from Kentucky.

There is a very fine line between success and failure. What is success to one may be failure to someone else. The successful venture or life may be rooted as much in attitudes as in the product or perception of what has actually been achieved. The ability to determine the needs of a community and to relate to the members of a community seem vital. The building of individuals by helping them raise their self-esteem is essential to success. If individuals can be part of the process of setting goals and feel necessary in the process of achieving these goals, success will be achieved. Success is in the eye of the beholder. Higher levels of leadership help individuals and communities set higher goals and focus more clearly on outcomes. This type of visionary concentrates on cooperation and a good blend of intrinsic and extrinsic rewards. There is an old adage that water seeks its own level. A successful leader requires that high expectations be set by the group, and then all work together to achieve those goals.

A director of curriculum from Louisiana, Wanda Gunn (personal communication, March 16, 1992), wrote about principles that guided her actions.

The principles that I have used to govern my administrative duties are fairness and timeliness, with no compromise on excellence. I believe in fairness for all those working within my supervision. Just as favoritism had no place in my classroom as a teacher, it has no place in my administrative working environment. I believe strongly that people do become what is expected of them. There is no place for procrastination in a successful administrative role. I believe that tasks, no matter how insignificant they might seem, should be completed on time and correctly. My staff is strongly encouraged to follow designated timelines, and I in turn follow up immediately on overdue assignments. I believe that a compromise on excellence is a compromise on character, whether as an individual or as an entire school system. When we accept mediocrity in education, we accept mediocrity as human beings. I believe that excellence should be the goal for all local, state, and national education.

Christine Johnson, (personal communication October 30, 1991), a high school principal from Colorado, described how she projected her vision.

I consider myself a visionary because I have a strong idea of what I would like [my school], and all schools, for that matter, to become. I realize that my vision alone will not guarantee the outcome I would like. I know that I must "sell" my vision and solicit the contributions and ideas of others. As a visionary, I see the importance of a shared vision as the guiding light for educational development. As a leader, I also see myself as a facilitator of this process. I view myself as a principle-centered leader. I have committed myself to doing what I feel is right as opposed to what is easy or traditional. Often this involves some risk taking and controversy; but I feel overall that a true test of my decisions and actions is how aligned these are with my principles.

Tenacity

An elementary school principal from Washington provided a model for tenacity. "I never give up, I do not take no for an answer. If you continually strive to get what you believe is good for your students and/or school, you will generally get what want you want. My superintendent always tells me he gives in to me just to get rid of me. I have always found that if I show him that it is good for my kids' school he will give in."

Honesty and Integrity

The irreplaceable characteristics of honesty and integrity were called to mind by a high school principal from Missouri.

When making school decisions, I have always tried to determine if what I think is best is truly in the best interest of the student(s). I feel I have an obligation to try to provide the best possible environment for students to work in. Basically, I'm honest to a fault and pretty much "tell it like it is." It has worked for me because people don't have to guess where I stand on issues. Also, I think an administrator needs to be a role model and stand for something. It's always tougher to take a position than it is to roll over; maybe that's the key.

A superintendent from Florida emphasized the importance of courage, integrity, trustworthiness, faithfulness, and justice.

I believe that if the traditional components of good character are missing, or are not husbanded within a person, then all the visible qualities that might be emulated will provide no more than short-term success, if any at all. I may be articulate, personable, able to inspire others with my words and ways. However, if I fail to show courage, to prove integrity, to be consistently trustworthy, faithful, and just, then I will lose my credibility as a leader, and others will turn away from me.

Commitment to the Profession

A philosophy of commitment to the profession was provided by a high school principal from Wisconsin.

My decision to enter the field of education and administration did not come easily. I struggled for quite some time deciding between education and the ministry. After finally making up my mind to go into administration, I knew I had made the right choice, and my commitment to the profession is now lifelong. In fact, I feel I actually have the best of both worlds because over the years I have come to the conclusion that there are a lot of similarities between a school administrator and a minister. Inherent in the word *administration* is the word *minister*. The responsibility of ministering to others is to counsel, to motivate, to listen, to nurture, to enhance, to criticize constructively, to sympathize, and to support in time of need. I love doing these things, and as a result, I thoroughly enjoy my work. I believe that the principal should make instructional leadership a priority. The principal needs to really know and understand the curriculum of his school. Curriculum should be discussed regularly with teachers, students, parents, school board members, and central office administrators. Instructional methods should be frequently reviewed and discussed with teachers. I think the principal should also stress academic achievement at every opportunity and publicly honor students for academic accomplishments. Finally, I am big on example and believe the principle should always work at setting a good example for students and staff. In most cases, I believe we teach what we are and not what we know. We need to take setting a good example seriously, especially in our dress, language, manners, attitudes, self-discipline, and organization.

Darrell Rud (personal communication, March 5, 1992), an elementary school principal from Montana, contributed his success in the profession of school administration to several factors.

I feel that I have been successful in my profession for the following reasons: (1) What I am doing is what I have always wanted to do. (2) I enjoy being in a profession that enables me to make a significant difference in many people's lives (both children and adults). (3) It has been my privilege to work in school districts that have high expectations and levels of support for me. (4) I have never been satisfied with just maintaining the status quo. I hope that I always remain visionary and progressive. (5) My belief in doing whatever is good for kids and the school requires me to give "over and above" minimum job requirements. The time and energy required are worth it. (6) I have had *many* opportunities to enhance educational opportunities for more children through active involvement at the city, area, state, region, and nation.

Hard Work

Judith Najib (personal communication, February 24, 1992), an assistant superintendent from Indiana, found no replacement for hard work.

A school administrator's success, as any individual's ultimate success, depends on hard effective work. It seems to have become a belief among some groups in this country that talent is all one needs to be successful. However, I believe that talent is not sufficient in itself. Hard work promotes achievement. Hard work requires us to be creative with what we know, compassionate in our actions, perceptive and eager to work with others, knowledgeable in our goals, content, and actions. We are educators because we believe in hard work. I have been successful because of the work ethic instilled in me by parents and educators.

A superintendent from North Dakota explained how hard work translated into leadership.

I am a real believer in the fact that school administrators must lead by example. I spend many hours on the job beyond what is required. We must model the level of energy, the attitude, and the commitment that we expect from our employees. I have always had a positive attitude and a lot of pride in accomplishment, two traits that I think are essential to a successful school administrator.

Risk Taking

In North Carolina, superintendent of schools C. Owens Phillips (personal communication, June 17, 1992) related why a risk he took about a controversial issue resulted in benefits for students.

Following is an example that demonstrates that I encourage people to take some risks and praise them for successes and support them particularly when they fail. Recently our board of education enacted a tough new policy against weapons in the schools that resulted in the suspension of more than thirty-five students for the remainder of the school year. Although the suspensions sent a strong message to students and the community about the commitment of the board and administration toward maintaining a safe and secure learning environment, it remained that thirty-five students were put out of school with no viable alternative education program. As members of our student services staff began to deal with the suspensions, they recognized the dangers involved in leaving students on the streets, some for as long as a year, where no positive influence could be made on their overall development and where there would be virtually no preparation for eventual reentry into the regular school setting. At that point, the associate superintendent for program services came to me with a proposal for a redirection program that would minimize educational loss for excluded students and work toward behavioral changes needed for successful reentry. The redirection program, she proposed, would be community based, offer a core curriculum, and also include intensive counseling, Saturday classes, and supervised community service. The program would be conducted in a local housing project away from any school campus and would require a commitment from the student as well as the parents in order to maintain eligibility. As superintendent I authorized her to proceed with planning as outlined; then I began a series of contacts with members of the school board, preparing them individually to receive the recommendation. The redirection program received mixed reviews throughout the school system and in the community at large. Those who had fought for a tough stance against weapons in the schools viewed the redirection program as a weakening of the policy. Some board members thought we were catering to students who break the rules and providing for them special attention and privileges not afforded regular students, such as one-on-one tutoring and individual counseling. Some suggested that housing all the "incorrigibles" in one setting would pose a threat to the safety and well-being of teachers and volunteers and to other tenants in the project. The program was studied and discussed at length in several public meetings of the school board and was the topic of several newspaper articles and editorials. The associate superintendent fielded a barrage of criticisms and objections to the program but adroitly adjusted criteria and provisions of the program where necessary to address and alleviate most concerns. All seven school board members were actively lobbied by the superintendent to support the new approach. Finally, the program was approved unanimously by the board and fifteen students were enrolled. Because of the nature of the program its chances for success cannot be guaranteed. However, the determination of these staff members to see that the program was offered if at all possible and their willingness to go the extra mile and to put themselves on the line on behalf of these students convinced me that the possibility that these young students could benefit from a second chance was *worth the risk* and *worth taking some "heat" over.* Importantly, the staff has had demonstrated to them in a tangible way that they have the support and encouragement of their superintendent to step out and search for new and different ways to help students succeed. They can feel comfortable in the future to put forth untested ideas and proposals without fear of rejection or repudiation . . . . As superintendent I have set certain expectations over the years that are ingrained in our operation. For instance, the decision to move forward with any program, whether new or ongoing, is subjected to the following question: "Is this likely to help students become successful?"

Role Models

From Wisconsin, a middle school principal noted the need for administrators to serve as role models in view of the many forces that impact upon schools and students.

I am a believer in change. Technology and change is happening so rapidly that we must continue to educate ourselves in the areas of greatest impact. More than ever, I feel we must be caring educators. We must work with developing a love for learning, respect for adults, and a work ethic in our students. We must be aware of the special needs of students and adapt our teaching to those needs. Principals are important role models, so as an administrator and building leader, I must set the best possible example to my students and staff. Finally, I believe in allowing school to be a place where learning can be interesting and fun. We need to motivate students to do the best they can do.

Ethics

John Spradling (personal communication, June 19, 1992), a junior high school principal from New Mexico, relayed his personal perspective about the need for ethical behavior and leadership in school administration.

The leaders in anything as with school principals must take the initiative to demonstrate, establish, and expect strong ethical behavior, ethical leadership concerned with fairness, consistency, commitment, responsibility, and so on, [that] are perhaps not a formal part of administrative training [but] can be developed and nurtured and best begun as an infant surrounded by a loving family . . . . In summation, the school principal must ever keep in mind that his mission is ultimately to educate human beings in an atmosphere of genuine caring, integrity, trust, listening, attention, and foresight with high expectations and a positive approach to life.

Respect for Ideas

A superintendent from Illinois wrote about an abstraction—a respect for ideas. The interrelationships among ideas, work ethic, and other factors are described in his response.

> My respect for ideas is pure. It is unbiased and unaffected by the source. It results in the impression that the individual is respected. Ideas and points of view must be heard and judged on their merit . . . . I think there is an integrity associated with that respect for ideas and also an integrity associated with my work ethic. For better or for worse, the job does come first, and I believe in taking on the tough jobs, persevering on those jobs, and maintaining what I believe is a high moral level of operating. Positions, rewards, criticisms, and assignments are based on merit, not on personal interests . . . . Perhaps the most important way to say it is that I believe in what I do and do what I believe in.

The value of research to teaching and learning was expressed by Art Feldman (personal communication, February 7, 1992), an elementary school principal from Wisconsin.

> Because we feel staff must be involved in the formation of the vision if we are to expect them to move toward implementation, we have a very active *School Effectiveness Team* . . . made up of teachers, educational assistants, and support personnel that helps chart the direction the school must go to provide quality education for our students. We think the challenge is clear. When research unmistakably tells us that the traditional procedure for teaching spelling, that is, the weekly word list featuring the Monday pretest and the Friday final test, is just a memorization exercise that does not transfer when the students write, why then is it so difficult to get teachers to find new ways to teach spelling? Too often, past practice continues far too long after we know it is ineffective . . . . We in the schools need to accept the responsibility to help our teachers learn how to teach using these "better" approaches . . . . I suspect some of my teachers, I hope the number is small, get a bit weary of my references to research and how we need to continually keep abreast of what it can tell us about how children learn. The SET is now deciding how we can do a better job of reporting student progress. As we were getting very close to making some important decisions, two second-grade teachers brought us all back to reality by asking, "What does the research say?" An excellent question.

The Nature of Success

Many beliefs, characteristics, attitudes, and values contribute to the success of school administrators. Perhaps the last word was provided by a high school principal from New York. He viewed success as a goal, a process, and an unattainable point of completion. Nevertheless, the process of striving toward the goal accounts for success along the way. "I believe success is a goal, a process, and it is what I strive for. I'm not there yet. I can see it, but it will and should, for me, remain just out of reach. It is the next application of research to better the students and profession, it is the next at-risk student who stays and graduates, it is the next teacher who takes a risk and grows and the support I give to make that happen."

SUMMARY

Now that you have read the comments on the educational philosophy of successful administrators, what conclusions have you drawn? Perhaps their thoughts, values, and insights provided you with inspiration, a desire for introspection about your own beliefs, and enthusiasm to serve your constituents but have not answered some questions, such as "How do I adapt and adopt their ideas into my own administrative and organizational leadership?" Perhaps the answer lies in the example provided by the respondents to Project Success: All considered what they thought contributed to their success and wrote accordingly.

Some wrote extensively; some submitted pithy statements almost jarring in their brevity. They wrote credos about their personal beliefs and values and about the value of holding fast and firm to them. Successful administrators made special mention of the value of public education to the United States.

When they wrote about schooling, particularly about academics, the respondents to Project Success adhered to the necessity of having a vision and of communicating their vision so that other members of the school community would support their vision. They also recognized that their responsibility for education extended beyond the borders of their own districts and sought to improve learning for all students, regardless of their place of residence. Successful administrators are compelled to continue the quest for excellence, to provide instructional autonomy to teachers, and to uphold quality education for all.

Learners, without question, are first priority. Successful administrators put the needs of students first, believe that all children can learn, incorporate learning styles into instruction, serve as advocates for children, and consider the developmental needs of students in curriculum and instruction.

Administrators who are eminently successful seek to create a positive school climate, work collaboratively with others, look for reasonable compromises, and embrace the concept of service to others. In decision making, administrators involve appropriate parties and pay great attention to developing positive interpersonal relations. Their leadership is predicated upon two principles: helping students learn and engaging all members of their administrative units in working toward a common goal. The demands of the 21st century focus continuous attention upon innovation and quality.

Respondents identified numerous attributes and characteristics that contributed to their success: being able to work well with others, having positive attitudes, setting high expectations for themselves and for others, being tenacious about meeting the needs of students, and having honesty and integrity. Also, as successful administrators they are committed to their profession; they are willing to work hard, take risks, and ready to accept the opportunity to serve as role models. Successful administrators act ethically and show respect for ideas, diversity, and others. They view success as a goal, a process, something to strive for along the way.

Perhaps you would have organized responses differently. For example, the subheading "Community" could have subsumed comments related to diversity, family, respect for others and expressly for students, the need for support from parents, and the contributions of teachers and other staff members. Respondents to Project Success wrote frequently about their learning communities; consequently, you may wish to search through administrators' comments for other themes. As you search for success in your profession, you will find it in the doing of your work—not at the end of your day or week but during the time you are striving to meet your ideals.

Each expectation you utter, each value you affirm, each attribute you model, and each action you take will advance you along the way to success. What you are and what you believe are evident in what you think, say, and do.

REFERENCES

Gardner, J. W. (1961). *Excellence, Can we be equal and excellent too?* New York: Harper.

Herrnstein, R. J., Murray, C. A. (1994). *The bell curve: Intelligence and class structure in American life.* New York: Free Press.

Smith, B. (1994). The Westside example: Facilitating high commitment. In J. M. Jenkins, K. S. Louis, H. J. Walberg, & J. W. Keefe (Eds.), *World class schools: An evolving concept* (pp. 41-48). Reston, VA: National Association of Secondary School Principals.

Why IQ isn't destiny. (October 24, 1994). *U.S. News & World Report, 117*(16), 73, 75-76, 78, 80.

Wraga, W. G. (1994). Performance assessment: A golden opportunity to improve the future. *NASSP Bulletin, 78*(563), 71-79.

2

VALUES

One of the most important components of an organization is the relationship of the personal values of decision makers to the values of their organization. Administrators are called upon formally and informally to articulate the values that undergird what the school stands for. In effect, values provide a kind of guidance system used by an individual when confronted with decision-making situations (Harrison, 1995).

A principal may try to shape the elements of school culture the way a potter shapes clay, patiently and with much skill (Greenfield, 1987). In this process, the principal articulates shared values, observes traditions and rituals, and significant school symbols. If the principal can express those values in a form that makes them memorable and easily understood, the school benefits from knowing what they stand for (Deal and Peterson, 1990).

The concept of values is an evasive one. Values mean different things to different people. Values may be regarded as the "normative standards by which human beings are influenced in their choice among the alternative courses of action they perceive" (Jacob, Flink, and Schuchman, 1962). Values may also be examined as "conceptions of desirable states of affairs that are used in selective conduct as criteria for preference or choice or as justifications for proposed or actual behavior . . . values are closely related, conceptually and empirically, to social norms" (Williams, 1967). "A value is an enduring belief that a specific mode of conduct or end-state of existence is personally or socially preferable to an opposite or converse mode of conduct or end-state existence" (Rokeach, 1973a).

Values are attitudes for or against some policies, programs, methods, practices, persons, places, things, events, and so on, which have a great influence on what the principals decide to accept or reject in their visions (McCall, 1994).

Deal and Peterson (1994) believe that "values are intrinsic qualities an organization stands for, what it considers good and important. Values are more intangible, less clearly delineated, and frequently expressed in abstract symbols or metaphorical stories. They can be interpreted in a variety of ways, giving them more elasticity and flexibility than concrete goals . . . and values often serve as goals to be achieved, ends to be attained."

EDUCATIONAL ADMINISTRATION AS A MORAL ENTERPRISE

Etzioni contended that what means most to people is what they believe, how they feel, and the shared norms, values, and cultural symbols that emerge from the groups with which they identify. He maintained that morality and shared values and commitments are far more important motivators than the basic, extrinsic needs and motives and even some intrinsic concerns (Etzioni, 1988).

Thomas Sergiovanni presented a case for the concept of value-added leadership. He contended that when moral authority transcends bureaucratic leadership in a school, the outcomes in terms of commitment and performance far exceed expectations (Sergiovanni, 1990).

Murphy (1992) called for preparation programs to have the goal of helping students articulate an explicit set of values and beliefs to guide their actions—to become moral agents. He based this goal on an extensive review of the literature on school administrator leadership. Crowson and McPherson (1987) stated, "The specific things (answers) that can be taught to prospective administrators may be less useful in many ways than a set of values behind the answers." Others also believe that educational administration is a moral enterprise. According to Hodgkinson (1978), administrative competence is of two kinds: (1) an understanding of organizations and organization theory and a knowledge of the theory and practice of decision making, and (2) a competence that divides into two areas; a capacity for logical analysis and a capacity for value analysis. With a capacity for value analysis, one is able to say, "The intrusion of values into the decision-making process is not merely inevitable, it is the very substance of decision" (Evers and Lakomski, 1991, p. 100). Greenfield (1991) puts it, "Values lie beyond rationality" (p. 13). Values can never be true or false, only good or bad, right or wrong. Hodgkinson (1978) says, "A value can exist only in the mind of the value-holder and it refers to some notion of the desirable, or preferred state of affairs, or to a condition which ought to be . . . . The objective terminology of science and logic deals with the true and the false. The subjective terms of value are 'good' and 'bad,' 'right' and 'wrong'" (p. 62).

LEADERS AND ACTIONS

What does this have to do with a school leader? It is the recognition that values are chosen and imposed. Educational administrators are constantly faced with choices among competing values; they have to make choices. These choices are moral ones. Whether they realize it or not, they choose among alternative values in the work they do and the actions they take. For example, what is good teaching? What is good policy? What is good management? What constitutes organizational improvement? How does education contribute to the community or to society? In answering such questions, administrators face the dilemma of choosing which values to subscribe to.

Today, educational administrators need to be competent in many areas. They need to be good managers, know budgeting, schedule making, and supervision, exhibit skills in technology and instruction as well as exhibit a host of skills that accompany the administrative trade. With the development of adequate instrumental skills comes administrative and personal competence; that is, instrumental skills are related to the development of an adequate self-concept. This is a necessary condition for values/ethical growth (Sullivan, 1994).

Values are communicated in everything a school leader does, writes, and speaks. This calls for a second set of skills that include the ability to be empathetic, to listen attentively, to pay attention to another, and to value others. Administrators must value student learning and growth and have convictions about the dignity and potential of every student.

Kouzes and Posner (1988), in surveying 1,500 individuals to determine what values (personal traits or characteristics) they admire in their superiors, found that followers admired leaders who were honest, competent, forward-looking, and inspiring.

VALUES OF ADMINISTRATORS IN THE STUDY

The outstanding administrators in this study had explicit value systems. They valued excellence, family, growth and development, a sense of community, a work ethic; they put students first, had integrity, were trustworthy and trusted others, empowered others, were sensitive, empathetic/forgiving, were good listeners, cared about others, had a belief in the contributions of others, and maintained a sense of humor. Much of what they conveyed can be termed a stage of transformational leadership, that is, leadership by building. "Here the focus is on arousing human potential, satisfying higher-order needs, and raising expectations of both leader and follower in a manner that motivates both to higher levels of commitment and performance" (Sergiovanni, 1991, p. 126).

A superintendent of schools from a large school district in Colorado reflected what many of the outstanding administrators were conveying when he said:

Effective leaders seem to have certain things in place. First, they are values oriented. To know what it is I value most gives me strength during times of adversity. It is essential that the effective leader be anchored and well grounded in terms of strong basic values. Perhaps it was said best years ago with the words "Know thyself." People will forever be pulling at you, in opposite directions, and absent a strong set of values, the administrator will forever be confused.

Do school administrators really hold these values, and more importantly, do they actually practice them? Those who are deemed outstanding certainly do. Let them tell you about the values they hold and give actual examples of their putting them into practice.

A Plethora of Values

A high school principal in South Carolina expressed her value system when she indicated that students were the most important people in her mind and, therefore, she must:

- be an advocate for students
- maintain integrity
- work harder than others
- take risks
- maintain high expectations
- treat all people in a fair, caring way
- care about my professional development and that of the staff
- be tolerant of others' views and opinions
- never sacrifice principles
- build leadership in the people with whom she works
- be a team player
- be open to change and help create a climate for change
- maintain a healthy sense of self and a "gigantic" sense of humor

Caring

A Minnesota high school principal, Richard Maas (personal communication, February 7, 1992), related that he looked forward to coming to work every day because he enjoyed working with people and helping young people obtain the best educational experience possible. Furthermore, he expressed the importance of care and concern for one another. "This caring atmosphere had a positive impact on the students, staff, and other adults." He related a favorite story to illustrate his caring and concern for others:

A most meaningful experience for me was my involvement with one of my students who was seriously injured in a car accident and lay in a coma in the hospital. I visited him weekly while he regained consciousness and endured a long therapy program. I encouraged students and community members to assist with a pancake breakfast to raise money to assist his family with the high medical bills.

Commitment to Excellence

An elementary school principal in Hawaii was representative of many of these outstanding school leaders and their commitment to excellence when she wrote, "What I do is based on my having high expectations and achieving them by collaborating with all involved. We keep striving to attain higher levels of achievement. High student achievement has played a large part in our school improvement plan."

The associate commissioner of education in Nebraska, Doug Christensen (personal communication, December 26, 1991), called for new schools for the 21st century if the United States is to remain in a role of international prominence. In his opinion, we do not currently have the kind of schools that will be needed for the 21st century. He calls for visionary leaders to step forward to "break the mold" and continually strive for excellence in our public education system.

An elementary school principal from Iowa told us that whatever success they had was centered around a drive for excellence. "My philosophy focuses on success, not failures, potential and not limitations, strengths and not weaknesses, and positive, not negatives."

Good Listener and Integrity

A superintendent of schools from a small rural school in Minnesota believed his success centered around the following: "I enjoy and respect other people as unique individuals. I try to be a good listener and give credit where credit is due. I care about kids, and they seem to understand this. I have integrity, and I am committed to my organization and generous with my time."

Work Ethic

A superintendent in Wisconsin felt his success was linked to hard work, dedication, and the practice of listening and involving people in the business of running the school. He said:

My sense is that by my working long hours, being active in as many district activities as possible, and using strengths of people within the organization, the message that work has a meaning and is valuable becomes obvious to others. The end result is that more and more people want to become part of a successful and forward moving organization; one that values its human resources more than its physical or financial resources.

A junior high school principal in Illinois shared the values that contributed to any success he may have had.

- Perseverance—Stick with it . . . . You must choose your battles. Learn to deal with ambiguity along the way.
- Integration—Question: do you know the difference between a job and a career? Answer: About twenty hours per week! Being an administrator means disregarding the clock. Your professional activities must blend with your family, social, and personal life.
- Enthusiasm—Project enthusiasm even when you least feel it. If you as a leader can't feel up and energetic about a project, how can you expect your followers to carry it through? Enthusiasm is contagious.
- Presentation—Look like a leader. Pay attention to your grooming and clothing because appearance leaves a strong impression. Dress the part of a professional. Would you trust a brain surgeon who wore hush puppies and a plaid polyester leisure suit?
- Prioritization—Keep your priorities straight. Just in case you're not certain what they are, here is my list: (1) health, (2) family, and (3) career.
- Sense of humor—Last of all, keep your sense of humor and don't take yourself too seriously. Enjoy what each day brings and be glad you're engaged in the most important endeavor imaginable.

Sincerity and Integrity

A principal of a middle school in Michigan believed his values of personal integrity and sincerity had served him well. He stated, "I am a person of integrity and sincerity. I believe that excellence leads to excellence. I set high standards for myself and expect my staff and students to do the same for themselves. I treat my staff as professional experts in their respective fields of study and value their knowledge and expertise when I make curricular and noncurricular decisions."

Openness, Trust, Respect, and Dignity

A highly successful superintendent of a large suburban school district in Colorado reported:

I believe my success was based on my reputation as an open and honest person whom people could trust. I tried to treat all people with respect and dignity. I did not take myself too seriously, often turning humor on myself. I concentrated on listening as much as speaking. In making decisions or settling differences, I tried to do what I believed was right and just, rather than cater to whom I could please or who might benefit. I spent about 100 hours a year in classrooms serving as a teacher's aide.

Caring and Sensitivity

Do school administrators really make a difference in the lives of the students they serve? Are they sensitive to students and really care about them and do students know they care? Don Briix, elementary principal in Harrah, Oklahoma (personal communication, March 23, 1992), shared this story as an example.

> I once had a fifth-grade student who came to my office, sat down, and told me that I had changed his life. This 11-year-old boy shocked me when he said, "You have changed my life." I remember sitting back in my chair waiting for him to tell me how and why I had changed his life. I was not used to students coming into my office and telling me I had changed their life. This boy had been in trouble many times with his teacher and in the classroom. He had been in my office many times for different problems. He told me he wasn't going to get into trouble any more with his teacher or in the classroom. He told me he was going to show her respect.
>
> He said that he told his mother that he knew that she was running around on his dad and he asked her to stop. He said that after he told her this she cried, took him into her arms, told him she was sorry and that she would stop.
>
> He said that what I did to change his life was that even when he was in trouble, I told him I cared about him and liked him but I didn't like the bad things he was doing. He said he knew that I wasn't just saying those words but that he knew I meant it. He said he learned how to care about others rather than just think about himself.
>
> This boy did straighten up. The teacher and he developed a positive relationship, his grades went up, and he wasn't sent to the office any more for discipline problems. He became a student of which his teacher, his parents, and I could be proud.
>
> That is what being an elementary school principal is all about!

EMPATHY AND FORGIVING

Outstanding administrators have empathy for students and others. They know that we are all human and that we make mistakes. Merry Wade, principal of a middle school in McPherson, Kansas (personal communication, June 17, 1992), said it best when she shared the following with us:

It's All Right To Make Mistakes

> I'd like you to picture a scene. There is mass confusion in a small room; from the back of that room a booming noise echoes as a stack of boxes falls to the ground; sheets of paper are flying in the air and fluttering

downward; in one corner, a child sits weeping; on a hard, wooden chair, a grown man sits with his head in his hands.

Is this the climactic scene from some Hollywood disaster movie? An air-raid shelter in a TV drama about a war? The part in a science fiction thriller where the aliens invade Earth? No, it is none of these. Rather, it is a fairly accurate description of what one classroom looked like some ten minutes after the opening of school on the first day of Jim's teaching career.

I grant you, that was some time ago and I was just a rookie principal, but the memory is crystal clear. If there is one thing teachers all have in common it is that memory of their very first day in the classroom.

On Jim's first day, however, I would not have given you two cents for Jim's chances of lasting out the week or my chances of helping him solve his problems. "Discouragement" was a positive word compared to how I felt as I dragged myself into the teacher's lounge at the end of that devastating day. I don't believe that I was ever at a lower point. Nothing had gone right—everything had gone wrong. Jim was a mess and I was speechless.

I suppose it must have shown, because Jim came over and sat by me. I had the mercy and sensitivity not to ask how he thought things had gone. He needed and wanted some kind of encouragement from me, the principal who had hired him. I don't know how long I sat there before I finally spoke to Jim. I said, "Jim, as I watched you today I remembered my very first day of teaching. It was an absolute disaster, but I did teach a very important lesson. I taught my students that it's all right to make mistakes."

"What?" He mumbled, coming out of his fog.

"That you can make mistakes and still learn," I continued. "I had passed out books and given an assignment before I realized that they were the wrong books, much too difficult for them. I had to collect the whole batch, put them away, get out the correct books, pass them out, record them all over again, reteach the lesson, and give a new assignment. It destroyed my entire morning schedule."

"But how did that teach them anything?" Jim asked.

"Because I told them that I had made a mistake. I told them precisely what I had done and asked for their suggestions as to how we could solve this problem. How we could put away the wrong books and get the right ones in the best possible manner. They told me; I listened; we did it, and everything went fairly well. After it was all straightened out, I thanked them for their help, and we had a very productive talk about what to do when you make a mistake. It was an excellent learning situation for them and for me."

"You mean," he stammered, "that you told them that you were wrong?"

"Jim," I responded, "that's what learning is all about. The willingness to say I made a mistake and can you help me."

DIGNITY AND RESPECT

How do school administrators practice the values of dignity and respect with students, and does it really make a difference? An elementary school principal in Columbia, Missouri, believes dignity and respect are the keys to helping young people. Listen to her story if you don't believe principals respect students and value dignity.

Dignity is a very personal, very important part of an individual. When dignity is taken away, an essential element of self-worth is going. Children begin to believe that they are bad, unworthy of receiving love, unable to learn, so they quit trying. Children then become what they think we think they are. I use every technique I can think of to get kids to believe they have control and power over themselves—dignity.

When a student returns to class after a "trip to the office," some staff members are unhappy if the child is not crying. Surely nothing good could have occurred if there's no physical evidence of punishment! In most instances, the child and I spend a great deal of time talking about what happened, how he or she reacted, what was gained or lost as a result of that action, and how a similar situation can be avoided in the future. I try never to ask why because why is usually an accusation, not a question.

I always ask, "How smart are you?"; the answer is almost always, "I'm smart." If it isn't, we work on that answer first! We then discuss how smart the action was. Usually, the child will say, "I didn't act very smart," then continue to tell me what should have happened instead.

I never raise my voice (a real challenge, sometimes), and I try to model for them the behavior they should display. I never degrade them—I want them to be able to maintain eye contact with me while we talk—because they want to, and not because I demand it.

When punishment is merited, I want students to know why and feel that it is fair. No student is punished in a way that will embarrass him or her in front of peers or adults.

To emphasize how she actually helps students maintain dignity and self-respect, she shared the following story.

Last week I had a fifth grader in my office who was sent by the teacher for "disrespectful behavior." He had torn up his math paper and thrown it away. I asked him if he was smart. He said he was. "Smart enough to learn to read your teacher?" His answer was, "I think so." I asked him what he learned about his teacher today. He said, "I learned that she doesn't like it when you tear up your paper and make a big deal about throwing it away" (a detail he hadn't mentioned before!). My next question was, "So?" To which he answered, "If I want to stay out of trouble I better not tear up my paper in her class. That makes her mad." That was the answer I wanted—he knows that he can control what happens to him if he learns what behaviors each of his teachers finds disruptive and then avoids them. If he can learn this skill successfully, he'll find a use for it the rest of his life.

FAMILY

With all the demands placed on school administrators for their time and energy, how do they find time for their own family? Do administrators value family and find ways to balance their life as an administrator and as a family member? It is difficult, but it can be done, as demonstrated by Barbara Zakrajsek, superintendent of a rural school in Minnesota (personal communication, April 8, 1992).

How does my family life, particularly as a single mother with three adopted daughters, help me to keep matters in perspective and remember what is important in life? The kids are the best part of my life. They make me laugh, they make me cry, and they make me slow down. They help me like the time when I came home from work totally exhausted and very sick—my 9- and 5-year-olds made supper, set the table, and even made special place mats. It was peanut butter and jelly sandwiches, but never have I dined better!

The kids give me an insight into what other parents feel and think. I try to keep my parent hat on when I am talking with other parents—it helps me to feel empathy. I also gain valuable instructional insights through my own children's teachers. My children allow me to be a child again. We read together and visit museums, art exhibits, and so on, together.

Another principal told us that since they had little social time outside of school, except for church, that he included his wife and family in as many school activities, functions, and duties as he possibly could. According to the principal, "This allows us all to grow together. I also encourage my staff to involve their families. This has helped our school family grow together."

AWARENESS

Sometimes administrators get so caught up in what they are saying that they overlook how they are saying it and how it is being perceived. Sensitivity and empathy are part of the value of awareness, a characteristic that helps refine what we mean by being able to put ourselves in someone else's position and feel what they are feeling. Outstanding school administrators balance awareness with a will for action, a resolution to move on while keeping everyone's needs in mind.

Sandra Looper, elementary principal in a rural Oklahoma community (personal communication, January 30, 1992), combines a number of values that she believes contribute to the success of her school. What stands out, however, is the manner in which she is aware of what is taking place in her school and is sensitive to the needs of students and faculty alike. She strives to build an atmosphere of trust and mutual respect. She is aware of the importance of faculty feeling good about themselves and having an opportunity to be involved and celebrate success. This is how she described her administrative style:

> I schedule regular small groups where teachers can comfortably express their concerns, ideas, and have input in school decisions. Individual grade-level meetings allow teachers an informal format where the principal has time to devote total concentration to the unique problems of a specific level. The intimacy of a small group also allows faculty to express concerns that may not be appropriate for a large-group meeting.
>
> During regular faculty meetings, I allow teachers to "shine" by allowing five to ten minutes in each faculty meeting for teachers to share something "extra special" that has worked well for them. In addition to having a good time learning together, that teacher is recognized and knows he or she is contributing to the success of the school. Encouraging adventurous techniques also sparks the rest of the faculty to take a risk and try something different. Assisting teachers to recognize their own talents and then highlighting and expanding them privately and publicly enhances both their personal and professional confidence.

Do you think Sandra Looper knows how to work with people and gain their support and trust? You can bet your last dollar she does! Not only does she know how to work with people, but she is aware of what is taking place in her school and what the faculty are doing.

Another way of expressing the value of being aware came from a Utah administrator who spoke of the need to be aware of the need for involving parents and the community with the schools. Furthermore, his value is based on the premise that as an administrator, we can never afford to get too far away from where learning is taking place. I feel that if we stay close to the classroom and close to those teachers, we can as administrators make decisions that will benefit everyone concerned. In my assignment in a large school district, our administrative team operates around the philosophy that input from the public and schools will lead to good decisions.

Marjorie Kaplan, superintendent of a unified school district in California (personal communication, November 5, 1991), was sensitive to how others perceive administrators. As a result, she substituted in the schools on a regular basis. Here is how she described her rationale for substituting on a regular basis:

Why do I substitute in the schools? I had always heard that district office administrators live in "ivory towers" and sensed that teachers and principals thought that we had forgotten what it is like to be in the classroom. I started my program of substituting to show them that I was not afraid to go out in the field. When I began substituting, however, I discovered a bonus. I was able to observe our students as they tried to learn; became thoroughly familiar with the programs that we offered; and really got to know teachers and principals. In addition to helping me make better decisions in many areas, including curriculum, instruction, and facilities, this simple program became an important part of a districtwide team-building effort.

STUDENT CENTERED—STUDENTS FIRST

Time and time again, we heard of school administrators who valued their students and told us that whatever else occurred, they put their students first. Patricia Popple, an elementary school principal in Wisconsin (personal communication, February 6, 1992), portrayed the sentiments of many administrators when she said, "I am concerned about children and find ways to get to their problems and to find solutions to meet their needs. I am child-oriented and concerned about my students."

As examples of her commitment to putting students first, she shared a number of stories with us. The following one best describes how one principal can make a difference in the life of a student.

When one child's parents didn't realize how much of a genius their little girl was, the counselor and I became her advocates. We advanced her to the next level, worked with her through some very tough times, and wrote letters to the school personnel in her next school to take special care to see that she was encouraged and allowed to pursue advanced materials. I hope someday we will see total success for this child. I still worry a lot about her and hope that someone will continue to be her mentor as she advances through school.

A high school principal in Louisiana said he always put kids first. "If you set this priority and work hard to achieve what is good for them, your school will be a winner! A principal must always remember that parents, superintendents, and communities want a good school first, not a good principal! However, if your school is a winner, they know you are responsible."

A principal from Bridgewater, New Jersey, James M. DeCicco (personal communication, February 4, 1992), shared a memo he sent to school staff that illustrates his commitment to students. It went like this:

Dear Staff:

Because we so easily get caught up in the less important or because we so easily busy ourselves with symbols, and scores, and keeping our heads above the flood of paperwork, we sometimes forget who we are and why we are here. So, I would remind you as I remind myself:

The most important people who enter this school's doors each day are not the principal, nor even the teachers.

The most important people who enter this school each morning are the *students*. Students are not an interruption of our work: they are the purpose of it.

Students are not cold statistics. They are sensitive young adults with feelings and emotions just like our own.

Students are young people who bring us their needs, and it is our responsibility to meet those needs professionally, courteously, and expeditiously. Teach and cherish them. That is why we are here.

HUMOR

It was surprising to see how many school administrators valued the use of humor. They felt it was important to not only laugh with others but to be able to laugh at themselves and not to take themselves too seriously. A number of administrators reported that it was especially gratifying to use light humor to break tension or to deal with a delicate situation. But as one administrator cautioned, "Be careful with and respectful of humor; don't try to make anyone look bad or be the butt of a joke."

Dennis Matthews, an administrator in Vancouver, Washington (personal communication, April 22, 1992), shared the following story that illustrates the use of humor.

I testified before the House Education Committee as a part of a panel. I noticed that my former high school teacher (a representative from eastern Washington) sat poised and ready for the panel's presentation; so I said, "I will approach this as an assignment. Let me know my grade." A few weeks later a member of the House staff wrote me a note: "You received an A minus. Call me and we'll talk about how you can get an A+!"

SUMMARY

School administrators constantly reflect their values in whatever they do. They must keep in mind that they are models others look to for leadership. They must keep in mind that their mission ultimately is to educate human beings in an atmosphere of genuine caring that puts students first. They must value hard work and exhibit trust, good listening skills, respect, sensitivity, and empathy. They must put people first. They must also have integrity and value excellence. Yet they must balance these values with a respect for family life and a drive toward professionalism. Throughout they must maintain a sense of humor.

The outstanding administrators cited here exhibited a positive way of viewing the world, yet had a firm set of beliefs, were open to change, and translated their values into positive action.

Perhaps one of the most sage responses we received came from a now-retired educator from Oklahoma. She succinctly stated that her personal creed was "to treat others the way you like to be treated." Sounds familiar, doesn't it? That universal value came through over and over again as we heard from outstanding administrators. This same educator told us what all educators need to keep in mind as they go about the profession of providing quality education for all children and youth: She reminded us that although there is a lot of ignorance in the world and we won't be able to erase all of it . . . we can sure make a dent wherever we are. Don't forget that we are dealing with our most valuable resource: the human mind!"

"Remember that people send you the very best kids they have—if they had any more, they would send them too. And don't forget, they want them back better than they were when you got them!"

REFERENCES

Crowson, R. L., & McPherson, R. B. (1987). The legacy of the theory movement: learning from new tradition. In J. Murphy & P. Hallinger (Eds.), *Approaches to administration training in education*. Albany, NY: SUNY Press.

Deal, T. E., & Petersen, K. D. (1990). *The principal's role in shaping culture*. Washington, DC: Department of Education, Office of Educational Research and Improvement.

Deal, T. E., & Peterson, K. D. (1994). *The leadership paradox: Balancing logic and artistry in schools*. San Francisco, CA: Jossey-Bass.

Evers, C., & Lakomski, G. (1991). *Knowing educational administration*. Oxford: Pergamon Press.

Etzioni, A. (1988). *The moral dimension: Toward a new theory of economics*. New York: Free Press.

Greenfield, T. (1991, April). *Reforming and revaluing educational administration: Whence and where cometh the Phoenix?* Chicago: American Association of Educational Research.

Greenfield, W. (1987). "Moral imagination and interpersonal competence: Antecedents to instructional leadership." In W. Greenfield (Ed.), *Instructional leadership*. Boston, MA: Allyn and Bacon.

Harrison, E. F. (1995). *The managerial decision-making process*, 4th ed. Boston, MA: Houghton Mifflin.

Hodgkinson, C. (1978). *Towards a philosophy of administration.* Oxford: Basil Blackwell.

Jacob, P. E., Flink, J. J., & Schuchman, H. L. (1962, May). Values and their function in decision-making. Supplement to the *American Behavioral Scientist 5.*

Karp, H. B., & Abramms, B. (1992, August). Doing the right things. *Training and Development.*

Kouzes, J. M., & Posner, B. Z. (1988). *The leadership challenge: How to get extraordinary things done in organizations.* San Francisco, CA: Jossey-Bass.

McCall, J. R. (1994). *The principal's edge.* Princeton, NJ: Eye on Education.

Murphy, J. (1992). *The landscape of leadership preparation: Reframing the education of school administrators.* Newbury Park, CA: Corwin Press.

Rokeach, M. (1973a). *Beliefs, attitudes and values.* San Francisco, CA: Jossey-Bass.

Rokeach, M. (1973b). *The nature of human values.* New York: Free Press.

Sergiovanni, T. J. (1990). *Value-added leadership: How to get extraordinary performance in schools.* New York: Harcourt Brace Jovanovich.

Sergiovanni, T. J. (1991). *The principalship: A reflective practice perspective,* 2nd ed. Boston, MA: Allyn and Bacon.

Sullivan, L. A. (Ed.). (1994). *The principal as leader.* New York: Macmillan College Publishing.

Williams, R. M., Jr. (1967, May). Individual and group values. *Annals of the American Academy of Political and Social Science.*

3

VISIONARY
LEADERSHIP

Considerable attention has focused on the leadership roles of politicians, and officials in nearly any organization. Emerging from this focus has been a renewed interest in examining the impact a leader's vision has on an organization. Literature has been generated from many sources, including business and education, to look at the role of visionary leadership in providing direction for the organization. Looking at organizations as cultures, two teams of researchers, Deal and Kennedy (1982) and Bennis and Nanus (1985), studied companies and their leaders. Their findings, which explain success and high performance in the business realm, are applicable to school organizations.

Successful companies are characterized by prominent values and beliefs that are freely articulated by members and affect their performance. These values and beliefs form an explicit philosophy assertively communicated by the leadership and shared by all members of the organization (Deal and Kennedy, 1982). Innovative organizations have a highly developed sense of purpose, and the energies of all members are aligned for the accomplishment of a desired future state (Bennis and Nanus, 1985).

Company leaders who achieve legendary fame are intuitive, persistent heroes driven by a desire to create, to defy order, and to realize a vision that in time proves to show prophetic wisdom. They incorporate their vision into the company's culture by getting others to own the vision. The attention devoted to the business world and the U.S. economy provided impetus for a book titled *Visionary Leadership*, (Nanus, 1992), which captured a renewed interest in leadership.

VISIONARY LEADERSHIP IN EDUCATION

The business world is not the only profession looking at leaders and organizations. Some of the research that helps us understand visionary leadership in education is that of Blumberg and Greenfield (1980), Lightfoot (1983), and Manasse (1986), who noted that outstanding principals were individuals whose commitment to their own beliefs about students, learning, or educational purposes was clearly perceptible.

Not only do visionary principals have strong personal convictions, but they work proactively toward realizing school goals consistent with their own beliefs and values (Blumberg and Greenfield, 1980; Deal and Peterson, 1990; Lightfoot, 1983).

Schools and corporations led by visionary leaders are characterized by observable manifestations of commitment to a shared ideology (Bennis and Nanus, 1985; Deal and Kennedy, 1982; Deal and Peterson, 1990; Kottcamp, 1984; Lightfoot, 1983). They recognize the powerful influence of ideology and effectively use cultural processes to create a shared ideology.

Visionary leaders are often identified as being innovators or risk takers, individuals driven by a desire to create new directions and new actions rather than to perpetuate the status quo (Bennis and Nanus, 1985). Their vision proves to show almost prophetic wisdom (Bennis and Nanus, 1985; Blumberg and Greenfield, 1980).

An unbridled pursuit of a better future drives the leadership actions of visionary leaders (Bennis and Nanus, 1985; Blumberg and Greenfield, 1980). Such leaders imagine the future of their organization as better than the present.

In contrast, nonvisionary leaders are concerned more with stability than with change. Their leadership style focuses upon maintenance and smooth operation of what is, rather than the motivation to visualize and achieve long-range purposes. Wolcott (1973) and Bredeson (1985) presented evidence of a managerial style in the thinking and actions of nonvisionary school leaders. These leaders focused on immediate events and maintaining daily order and lacked vision for the future.

One of the best summaries of research on visionary educational leadership is presented by Grady and LeSourd (1990). They brought together for examination the research on leadership in school and leadership in corporate settings. Close scrutiny led them to the conclusion that a common link was a leadership ideal that emerged each time leaders were identified as such. They termed this leadership type visionary leadership. According to LeSourd and Grady (1990), five prominent attributes emerged from their review of the research. These characteristics represent a leadership ideal closely related to vitality and improvement in the life of a school and thus represent their conceptualization of visionary leadership for school administrators. The five prominent attributes are as follows:

- First, visionary administrators have strong personal convictions to which they are enthusiastically committed.

- Second, visionary administrators work vigorously toward realizing goals in the school that are consistent with their personal convictions.
- Third, visionary administrators treat the school organization as a culture with traits and processes that are to be skillfully employed in efforts to effect change.
- Fourth, visionary administrators gain reputations as innovators because they assertively initiate new actions and new directions for their school.
- Fifth, visionary administrators have a personal image of their school in the future. The imagined school of the future is better in some ways than the school of the present.

WHAT IS A VISION?

Webster's New Collegiate Dictionary (1977, p. 1308), provides several definitions for vision: (1a) something seen in a dream, trance, or ecstasy; (1b) an object of imagination; (1c) a manifestation to the senses of something immaterial. (2a) the act of power of imagination; (2b1) mode of seeing or conceiving; (2b2) unusual discernment or foresight; (2c) direct mystical awareness of the supernatural in visible form. (3a) the act of power of seeing; (3b) the special sense by which the qualities of an object (as color, luminosity, shape and size) constituting its appearance are perceived and which is mediated by the eye. (4a) something seen; (4b) a lovely or charming sight.

Most people can recall their childhood dream of what they wanted to be when they grew up. Many remember when they fell in love, married, and imagined the life they hoped to build with their mate. Perhaps you can recall these or the dreams and hopes you formed when you started out in your career or joined an organization. If you can remember your early hopes and aspirations, you have a good idea of what a vision is. These same concepts apply to leaders as they join together with other individuals for some common purpose. A leader's vision inspires action and helps shape the future by the effect it has on others.

Nanus (1992) said that quite simply, a vision is a realistic, credible, attractive future for your organization. It is a manifestation of a destination toward which you and your organization should aim, a future that in important ways is better, more successful, or more desirable for your organization than is the present.

Vision deals with the future because it expresses for those who share the vision what they will be working hard to create. Not everyone thinks about the future, but those who do help shape the future. As such, a vision is only an idea or an image of a more desirable future for an organization, but it can energize people by utilizing the talents and skills of an organization to make it happen. Today, new paradigms are called for as we move into the 21st century. People with vision will help usher in "new" products and organizations that will lead the way. President John F. Kennedy's dream for putting man on the moon in the 1960s or Martin Luther King's famous "I have a dream" speech are examples of individuals having vision.

Vision is not only important in the planning and startup phase of an organization or enterprise but imperative in keeping the dream alive through its constant application. Every organization at some time needs redirection or a transformation that requires a new vision. Thus vision is central to leadership and is the ingredient without which an organization is doomed to failure.

VISION IN ACTION

The true test of a leader is selecting, articulating, and getting others to share the right vision. The realization of the dream is well underway when this happens. The right vision demands a commitment and renews an organization. People need challenges; and for an organization to be truly effective, a commitment must be made by all, not just the leader. A vision creates meaning in the lives of those involved whereby they view themselves as important cogs in the organization and members of the team, not just merely workers. Pride, self-image, and a feeling of ownership are strong motivators for individuals involved. A standard of excellence is also established by vision. Basically, people want to do a good job, and when they feel they are part of the organization and share in the accomplishments, the level of competence is likely to rise. Vision is necessary to bridge the present and the future of an organization. The right vision encourages long-range planning and a forward-looking attitude whereby the organization is constantly evaluating itself and working to elevate the organization to the next level.

The vision is the guiding light of an organization's future. People who share the vision are empowered to plan and take actions that advance the vision, being assured that such actions will be valued by all who share the dream.

Can an organization survive without a vision, or is it destined to perish? Few organizations can go on year after year repeating the same things over and over. Change is inevitable, and a visionary leader will emerge or the organization will go down the tubes.

In the end, organizational behavior is shaped by a shared vision of a better future. Developing, sharing, and shaping such a vision is imperative for school leaders, for people will follow the leader who follows the dream. Walt Disney has often been quoted as saying, "If you can dream it, you can do it!" If a school administrator can dream it and share that dream with others, schools can do it.

THE VISIONARY SCHOOL ADMINISTRATOR

What does this thing called vision have to do with successful school administrators? Why has so much attention been given to visionary leadership? Do successful school administrators really have a vision and work with others to make that dream an integral part of quality education?

Nanus (1992) emphasized there is no more powerful engine driving an organization toward excellence and long-range success than an attractive, worthwhile, and achievable vision of the future, widely shared. No discussion of outstanding school administrators would therefore be complete without attention to vision, a key ingredient of leadership in highly successful organizations (Peters and Waterman, 1982). In contrast to the executives of Japanese corporations, who plan 250 years into the future, executives in the United States seldom plan for the far future. School administrators, however, had better have a vision for their schools.

Visionary leadership is a prominent trait of high-performing administrators. The U.S. Department of Education's *Principal Selection Guide* (1987) states that "effective school leaders have broad visions that are clear, active, ambitious, and performance-oriented." The *Guide* further notes that effective administrators "create conditions to help them realize their visions." Vision is the force that propels effective administrators to strive to shape their individual schools for success.

In the National Association of Elementary School Principals (NAESP) *Principals for 21st Century Schools* (1990), a number of characteristics are enumerated for effective leaders, one of which is "has a vision and leads toward that vision." Indeed, a crucial aspect of leadership is the development of a vision that not only calls for excellence but establishes an educational environment and culture in which this can be achieved. Administrators must be willing to ask "What are we doing? Is it working? Can it be done better?" and then listen to the answers. Administrators who are leaders must be able to model and articulate their visions while striving to actualize the organization they envision (Chance and Grady, 1990).

A vision unifies a school and increases the emotional support of those in the organization (Littky and Fried, 1988). Vision begins with the individual and totally guides those who are involved in a school. Vision helps establish the climate for the school because when the vision is clear and shared, expectations, purposes and goals are clear.

VISIONARY LEADERS

School administrators without vision would be like sunshine without daylight, a swimming pool without water, or ice skating without ice! Effective administrators who are instructional leaders and utilize shared decisionmaking and team-building activities possess vision. A priority of a school administrator must be the creation, articulation, and development of a vision for the school. Vision provides the ultimate set of goals and when a visionary leader shares the vision with others in the school, the journey of leadership can be exciting and extremely rewarding.

Simply put, the successful effective school administrator must develop, implement, and sustain the vision of not just what the school *should be* but what the *school will be*! How did the outstanding school administrators identified in Project Success feel about vision and visionary leadership? Here is what they told us.

When respondents identified "vision," they spoke of personal and professional goals, a picture of the future, clearly written statements, a global perspective, mission, the 21st century, and networking. Marshall McLuhan prophesied the coming of the "global village." It is here already? Contrast the image of the little red schoolhouse snugly nestled among the pines with classrooms globally linked through satellites, fax machines, telephones, distance learning options, fiber optics, and the like.

Cynthia Grennan (personal communication, March 5, 1992), superintendent of a California unified school district, had this to say about vision: "I believe I understand what an effective school system looks like and have the ability to communicate that vision throughout the organization . . . along with an accompanying sense of urgency with respect to getting there. I am also optimistic, arrogant, naive enough to think that I can help to move the school system from where it is to where it ought to be."

Do teachers understand and appreciate an administrator who exhibits vision and practices visionary leadership? A middle school teacher in Washington described her principal as follows: "The principal's vision of a community of leaders evolved out of a judgment that the school could be changed for the better." Given the desire to pursue a more desirable alternative, relative to what she observed, the principal then acted to realize those objectives. She had to articulate the vision to others and move them to action. "Because school is essentially a social situation, the principal's primary means of influencing what happened at IMS was to work with and through the entire IMS school community."

The principal as instructional leader is a key component in most principals' job descriptions. Art Feldman (personal communication, February 7, 1992), an elementary principal in Wisconsin, related his vision to being an instructional leader:

The principal, as the instructional leader, needs to have a vision. It is not enough to simply relate this vision to staff; we must have the resources of time, money, and commitment to cause it to become a reality. At our school, the staff has the opportunity to get fifteen hours of individual inservice training each year to pursue their special areas of interest. As chairperson of the inservice committee, it is my job to oversee this activity and, in fact, make sure that staff are aware of the great many opportunities that are available to them. I feel so strongly about staff development that staff can attend workshops and conventions even if school is in session. They not only receive their salary for the day but are reimbursed for their expenses.

A Nebraska superintendent of schools, Fred Bellum (personal communication, November 4, 1991), strongly believes an administrator must have a vision for the school district that is focused on student and staff growth and development. He was kind enough to share his personal vision, which is widely known in his district. "The superintendent's vision is a district where all students meet selected outcomes because each student is actively engaged in learning an objective selected at the correct level of difficulty using instructional materials designed by a teacher knowledgeable of the instructional process. This will take place in good facilities with adequate financial and support services. The educational program will reflect strong community involvement." This vision has served the superintendent well for over nineteen years in the same school district. He also indicated that he worked hard to ensure that others, including the community as a whole, had opportunities for input into the district planning process.

An elementary school principal in Columbia, Missouri, expressed the need for a vision as follows: "After establishing the sense of community, we work on developing our vision of what can be. We then plan strategies that will lead to the attainment of objectives, goals, and the vision. At this point, the administrator becomes a facilitator, counselor, and cheerleader. A key administrative behavior is knowing when to get out of the way and when to guide."

A superintendent in Alabama, Cleveland Hammonds (personal communication, March 11, 1992), described the need for vision by reporting, "A plan or vision must be developed in a manner that gives the community and the system a feeling of ownership. Once the vision is in place, it is my job to make the tough choices, realizing that not everyone will agree with them, but everyone realizes what must be done because we have a shared vision."

"I consider myself to be a visionary because I have a strong idea of what I would like . . . high schools, and all schools, for that matter, to become," expressed Christine Johnson (personal communication, September 30, 1991), a high school principal in Colorado. "I realize that my vision alone will not guarantee the outcome I would like, but without a vision, what guides us to reach even farther? I know that I must sell my vision and solicit contributions and ideas of others if it is going to be meaningful. As a visionary, I see the importance of a shared vision as the guiding light for educational development. As an administrator, I see myself as a facilitator of this process."

A middle school principal in Kansas, Merry G. Wade (personal communication, June 17, 1992), stated, "I am an innovator and a visionary who is not content to focus on what is, but what can be. Children are the best students when they are on 'fire' with the job of learning, and it's teachers who set them blazing. My role is to have the vision to keep them challenged and moving forward."

The superintendent of a large school system in Kentucky viewed his role as a visionary to be key in the district. He stated, "Higher levels of leadership help individuals and communities develop a vision whereby they set higher goals and focus more clearly on outcomes. This type of visionary, in my opinion, concentrates on cooperation and a good blend of intrinsic and extrinsic rewards. There is an old adage that water seeks its own level. A successful leader helps require that high expectations are set by the group and then all work together to achieve those goals."

"We must be willing to lead the way down new paths and have a vision of something better for our schools," according to an elementary school principal in North Carolina. "Of course, visions and new ideas should be based on some type of research or intellectually sound reasoning."

A superintendent of a large school district in North Dakota, Mark Sanford (personal communication, March 26, 1992), stated that the key to his success is that he has worked hard to develop a vision for the district. He makes sure people understand it and are able to identify appropriate roles for themselves in the quest to fulfill the vision.

The need not only to have a vision but to articulate it clearly and share it with others was repeated time and time again by the respondents to Project Success. A Minnesota elementary principal, Robert Ziegler (personal communication, April 21, 1992), stated:

> I think I was identified as an outstanding administrator because I am able to articulate and communicate my vision for the school clearly to staff, parents, and students to bring about positive changes in our school. My vision of an ideal school is an environment in which all the parts work together; parents, teachers, administrators, staff, and students. It should be a place where kids feel good about themselves and realize they can be successful.

An elementary principal in Utah, Patti Harrington (personal communication, April 8, 1992), shared the view that a vision is important for a school as a whole; it is more than just the principal's vision. "Visions do not appear only to leaders of organizations. They may more readily appear to online workers who thoroughly understand their work and see new ways of applying old formulas. Empowering others to envision their best work is the job of a good leader."

Stuart Berger (personal communication, January 2, 1992), superintendent of one of the largest school districts in Kansas, talked about how commitment and vision must work together when he said, "I have used my commitment to form my vision. No leader can be successful without a vision, no matter how committed. Focusing a vision requires one to employ good people, give them the latitude to do their jobs, and hold them accountable."

A highly successful school leader in Nebraska felt so strongly about the need for vision that he expressed it by saying, "It is more important for leadership to be a vision builder than a management provider. Vision is about people and programs; management is about things and structures." He further stated that while leaders are responsible for being the catalyst to a vision-building process, they are not responsible for giving the vision to others. Instead, the vision-building process is best described as a process of "opening windows."

A superintendent of a large school district in Colorado, Harlan Else (personal communication, February 13, 1992), believes it all begins with a vision.

> I believe it's important to paint pictures in people's minds. I use my own visual capabilities to talk about concepts in terms of colorful and descriptive language rather than simply providing data. For example, I like our board to have a real vision about the budget rather than just thinking of the budget as numbers that relate to revenue and expenditures. I have renamed revenues as "resources" and expenditures "investments." I ask board members to picture the kids in Mrs. Smith's first-grade classroom at [an] elementary school sitting around a table learning to read; or

Mrs. Green's third-grade students at [a] school in the computer lab using technology to learn a math skill. Each of these pictures is an investment of our precious financial resources in the future of the kids in our district.

An elementary school principal in North Carolina described his role as a principal as follows: "The essence of being a principal is that it is not a position of power or authority but an opportunity to help define and to help refine. It is an opportunity to share a vision and perhaps create a new vision, based on the visions of the many."

A clear vision of educational excellence has to be in place to enable personnel and students to understand their mission and role in the continuing pursuit of excellence," according to a superintendent in one of California's largest districts.

"My role as a school leader is to transmit an overall shared vision centering on the basic belief that all children can learn," related a large-school superintendent in North Carolina. A five-year curriculum plan for the district resulted from this vision.

A high school principal in Kentucky indicated that a vision was important to shape the destiny of the school. "I believe that we can shape the destiny of the school. According to him, "I believe that we can shape the future, rather than allow it to control us. To do this we have to share a vision of what can be and take the necessary risks to be change agents to meet the needs of students for the future."

James H. Fox, Jr. (personal communication, February 5, 1992), superintendent of a large school district in Georgia, expressed, "A shared vision is the key to success. We need to know where we are going and how to know when we get there. People need to understand the direction in which the district is traveling and what benchmarks to look for when parts of that vision are accomplished."

"It all begins with a clear and compelling vision that is shared by all," according to a middle school principal in Florida. "I believe that an effective school administrator must be a visionary, a risk taker, and lead through example."

Dolores A. Ballesteros (personal communication, November 11, 1991), a superintendent from California, said she has been told by colleagues, "You are a visionary who can share that vision with others and get them to follow." She feels that a key to her success has been her vision for a holistic approach to education that has been recognized and appreciated by the community.

SUMMARY

The successful school administrators in our study have no doubts that being a visionary is necessary for effective schools. One after another, school administrators stated that the way to success begins with a vision based on personal beliefs and values. Commiting oneself to that vision and sharing it with others are necessary to further refine and shape the vision into specific goals for the school. Everyone comes to understand where the school is going, that is, what its aims are, and what the school will be like when those aims are reached. Furthermore, putting a vision into action by being an innovator and a risk taker, initiating change and always looking to the future and what can be, is common among successful school administrators as they work with staff, parents, students, and the community.

This story from an elementary school principal in Alabama exemplifies the impact visionary leaders have on others. As you read, think about the vision this principal had based upon her personal beliefs and values.

> Michael was a fourth grader in our school. His teacher asked me to intervene when she intercepted a note he had written. In the note, he had used the word *nigger*. As the teacher was black, she had a lifetime of hurtful memories attached to this term. Under our board policy I could have paddled Michael or administered other punishment in the name of discipline. Instead I chose not to discipline him but to teach him. I took Michael to the library, had him check out the book, *Roll of Thunder, Hear My Cry*, and asked his parents to read it to him. For the next several days, I conversed with Michael in a friendly way about the book. After they had finished reading it, his mom came to school asking to share her feelings, saying she had been too casual about understanding black history. If I had been harsh with Michael, he and possibly his parents would have been angry with me. Since I taught them instead of punishing them, they could use their energies to look at the significance of using the word *nigger*. My goal was to teach through respect and love. Understanding Michael as a child of the 1990s helped me adapt discipline in an appropriate, effective way. He and his family cooperated and thanked me for helping them.

REFERENCES

Bennis, W., & Nanus, B. (1985). *Leaders: Strategies for taking charge*. New York: Harper and Row.

Bloom, A. (1987). *The closing of the American mind: How higher education has failed democracy and impoverished the souls of today's students*. New York: Simon and Schuster.

Blumberg, A., & Greenfield, W. (1980). *The effective principal: Perspectives on school leadership*. Boston, MA: Allyn and Bacon.

Bredeson, P. V. (1985). An analysis of the metaphorical perspective of school principals. *Educational Administration Quarterly, 21*, 29-50.

Chance, E. W., & Grady, M. L. (1990, November). Creating and implementing a vision for the school. *NASSP Bulletin*.

Deal, T. E., & Kennedy, A. A. (1982). *Corporate cultures: The rites and rituals of corporate life*. Menlo Park, CA: Addison-Wesley

Deal, T. E., & Peterson, K. D. (1990). *The principal's role in shaping school culture*. Washington, DC: U.S. Department of Education.

Grady, M. L., & LeSourd, S. J. (1990). Principal's attitudes toward visionary leadership. *The High School Journal, 72* (2) 103-110.

Kimball, R. (1990). *Tenured radicals: How politics has corrupted higher education.* New York: Harper and Row.

Kottkamp, R. B. (1984). The principal as cultural leader. *Planning and Changing, 15,* 152-160.

LeSourd, S. J., & Grady, M. L. (1990). Visionary attributes in principals' descriptions of their leadership. *The High School Journal, 72* (2), 111-117.

Lightfoot, S. L. (1983). *The good high school: Portraits of character and culture.* New York: Basic Books.

Littky, D., & Fried, R. (1988, January). The challenge to make good schools great. *NEA Today.*

Manasse, A. L. (1986). Vision and leadership: Paying attention to intention. *Peabody Journal of Education, 63,* 150-173.

Nanus, B. (1992). *Visionary leadership.* San Francisco, CA: Jossey-Bass.

NAESP. (1990). *Principals for 21st century schools.* Alexandria, VA: National Association of Elementary School Principals.

Peters, T. J., & Waterman, R. H., Jr. (1982). *In search of excellence.* New York: Harper and Row.

Sykes, C. (1988). *Profscam: Professors and the demise of higher education.* Washington, DC: Regnery Gateway.

U.S. Department of Education. (1987). *Principal selection guide.* Washington, DC: U.S. Department of Education.

Webster's new collegiate dictionary. (1977). Springfield, MA: Merriam-Webster.

Wolcott, H. R. (1973). *The man in the principal's office: An ethnography.* New York: Holt, Rinehart and Winston.

4

INSTITUTIONAL LEADERSHIP

Outstanding school leaders value the opportunity they have to institutionalize a part of their contribution. They believe in public education; they recognize the institution has been instrumental in providing the caliber of individuals who have made this country the strongest, most successful, most imitated, and most compassionate country in the world. They recognize that if the country is to remain strong, it must constantly provide more inspired, more motivated, more willing individuals who move humankind forward. Outstanding leaders recognize the vital role they play in making the country strong, and they welcome the opportunity and the obligation to do so.

THE ROLE OF EDUCATION IN AMERICA

The world is changing dramatically. Walls are coming down and iron curtains shredded. Tyranny is being silenced, and even the most stubborn dictators are losing their confidence and power. American blue jeans, Nike® shoes, and American music are becoming as much of an icon as the Statue of Liberty. Democracy is hailed universally to set people free.

The Founding Fathers consistently acknowledged the need for an educated citizenry for the preservation of democracy. Yet endless criticism of education is evidenced in recent books that prefer to damn democracy and education rather than praise it. For example, Allan Bloom's *Closing of the American Mind*, Charles J. Syke's *Profscam*, and Roger Kimball's *Tenured Radicals* all link educational crisis with progressivism, equality, and radical professors.

Democracy is less the enabler of education than education is the enabler of democracy. At one time, the relationship was well accepted. Schools of all types (public, private, religious) espoused a common commitment to education as a concomitant of democracy (Barber, 1992).

Theories of or views on the role of education abound. Some would argue that education's goal is to transmit the culture, whereas others would say the purpose of education is to develop the individual. Still others make the argument that culture shapes education. Whether aware of it or not, school administrators represent in their thinking and actions a blend of these theories. School administrators as institutional leaders have responsibility for an institutional process that has a purpose. The way this job is undertaken and accomplished directly relates to that purpose (Lane and Walberg, 1987).

The relationship between schools and society is characterized by three roles that reflect philosophical viewpoints: *reproduction, readjustment,* and *reconstruction* (Johnson, Collins, Dupuis, and Johansen, 1988). The reproductive role is the transmission and preservation of the existing culture, values, traditions, and norms. The readjustment role involves responding to changes in society and adjusting education accordingly. The reconstruction role is expressed as one by which schools are agents of societal change. These three roles have been carried out by means of school purposes and goals that are classified as political, social, economic, vocational, intellectual, and personal (Goodlad, 1984; Spring, 1991).

Where do school administrators come into play in the scheme of education and society? How important are school administrators in shaping the philosophy and actual operation of the school? Kolwalski and Reitzug (1993), made a strong case for the importance of school administrators when they stated, "Similar to the interrelationship between schools and society is the interrelationship between administrators and their schools. Administrators both shape their school's philosophy and purpose and are shaped by it as well as by society."

Barber (1992) believes that the fundamental task of education in a democracy is the apprenticeship of liberty—learning to be free. He believed that in democracies, education is the indispensable concomitant of citizenship. Where women and men would acquire the skills of freedom, it is a necessity.

LEADERS OF AMERICA'S SCHOOLS

What did these outstanding school leaders believe about the role of education in a democratic society? Are they committed to the cause of universal education for all students? Do they really believe every child counts and can learn? The school leaders identified in this study were adamant in their conviction that the school was the foundation of American society. There is no doubt they took their responsibilities seriously in wanting to provide in their community and in their schools the best possible education for all children. Here are some representative comments from these outstanding school leaders.

COMMITMENT

The retired superintendent of the Lincoln, Nebraska, public schools, John Prasch (personal conversation, 1991), probably summarized it for all school leaders when he responded, "I attribute whatever success I have had as a school administrator to a commitment to public education, bordering on missionary zeal, based on my conviction of the importance of preserving the concept of the 'common school' as a unifying power in an ever more pluralistic society, the only vehicle that ensures the economic and social mobility necessary in a democracy, along with the necessity to provide equal access to quality education for all children." What a powerful commitment to public education! Other comments by school leaders may not have been as eloquent as those of John Prasch, but they reflect the same commitment to the necessity of education. A superintendent of Schools in Martinsville, Indiana, James L. Auter (personal communication, November 26, 1991), expressed it thus: "I believe that schools can make a significant difference in the progress of our society. The stakes are very high and further change is required. It is our opinion that our carefully developed educational philosophy should serve as our vision and guide as we participate in the improvement and restructuring process. Change will not come through coercion, nor command and control, but through carefully planned processes that develop collaboration and networking."

PUBLIC SCHOOL ADVOCACY

James D. Buchannan (personal communication, December 3, 1991), superintendent of the Tempe Union High School District responded: "I come from a family of educators and was literally born to be a school person. In my family, the American Common School is considered the greatest single institution ever invented. It's not hard for me to be an outspoken advocate because I was raised to believe it from a very early age. I find, however, that advocacy is most effective when the advocate recognizes what is wrong as well as what is right. I am never defensive about the ills plaguing public schools, but I always take a 'how do we get better?' approach."

Another superintendent from Arizona told us, "I practice a strong belief in the ideals of public education for the survival of our democracy." Likewise, a now-retired elementary school principal in Oklahoma said, "The public school is the first line of defense for democracy and democracy must be practiced in the principal's office." The principal of the Paducah Tilghman High School in Paducah, Kentucky, Florence B. Morton (personal communication, March 6, 1991), expressed a similar thought:

> I know the purpose of the school and adhere to the purpose. I keep in mind the objectives of the school: (1) to produce and to develop inquisitive and logical minds and (2) to prepare young people for an interesting and profitable life. I seem to organize the school so that the maximum utility

can be obtained from all personnel, individually and collectively . . . . Successful principals strive to be proficient in supervision and management of the schools they lead. They have vision for the school, its students and staff. They never stop learning, striving, and growing as a leader of leaders.

A state superintendent of public instruction shared his appreciation for public education when he said, "I believe service is what public education is all about; that when we commit our resources and energies to do the best we can for students, everyone benefits. Excellence really can be a state of mind, and many benefits can result from positive thinking. Basically, I enjoy helping people—especially children—feel good about themselves."

Another state superintendent for education stated, "I believe that education must provide opportunities for students to learn how to become contributing citizens. To learn how to get along with other people, to follow rules and regulations, to assume responsibility and respect others' rights, are as important today as in any period of time."

A former superintendent of schools who is now a college professor, Larry Dlugosh (personal communication, February 15, 1992), pointed out the importance of public education with this comment: "Many forces, internal and external, are trying to determine the fate of the American public school system. Some are legitimate; some are selfish and political. Public education remains a strong foundation for America. It needs advocates and friends who understand the power of learning and teaching all students; people who will help change them to meet new demands. I am privileged to count myself among them."

A superintendent of schools in Oregon described his commitment to public education as follows:

My enthusiasm for school administration and public education has increasingly heightened. Public education has been an awesome experiment and has, of course, been a cornerstone of America's development, and I appreciate that. More appreciated is the opportunity for the future. America and public education are truly at a paradigm shift as evidence by global influences, demographic changes, societal demands, proposals for school choice and vouchers, and changing expectations. What an exciting time! The paradigm shift I refer to centers on the necessity to move to a broadened sense of community. The school leader has an expanded community responsibility to rally and facilitate the entire community toward agreed-upon goals.

LEADERSHIP

The concept of leadership came to the forefront over and over as we looked at outstanding school administrators. Just what type of leadership was mentioned? How is it exhibited in the schools they lead? Here are some selected comments made by school leaders.

The superintendent of schools in Dover, New Hampshire, Gerald A. Daley (personal communication, February 24, 1992), wrote, "If I have had any success at all, it is because I believe a successful school administrator must be more than a good manager. He or she must be an educational leader. Educational leaders provide direction for their schools. They set goals and hold people accountable for reaching them. They have high expectations for both personnel and students. They care about people and they care about results."

The superintendent of the Wichita, Kansas, public schools, Stuart Berger (personal communication, January 2, 1992), expressed the view that "ultimately, if one stands for something, one finds decision making easy; one must determine whether a given action furthers the mission and decide accordingly. I am not arguing that successful administrators can ignore politics, but I believe doing what is right will prevail in the long run. It may not be easy, but it is almost always effective."

Superintendent of Schools Russell A. Joki of Tigard, Oregon (personal communication, October 17, 1991), succinctly said, "Leadership, I have found, is working with people and engaging them in thinking about planning and acting that, in the end, will be regarded as rewarding and productive. The spark is asking the right questions to the right people."

The principal of the Minot High School in Minot, North Dakota, Richard J. Olthoff (personal communication, January 16, 1992), believes his responsibility as a school leader is "to focus on and promote educational restructuring. I have a responsibility to have an impact on education. That can best happen if I promote instructional leadership and educational change for programs and activities."

A middle school principal in New Mexico, Cheryl Pongratz, (personal communication, February 8, 1992), sees the role of the principal thus: "Effective school administrators need to be able to create a feeling of belonging, involvement, and a sense of personal control among the school community: students, staff, and parents. Everyone involved with the school needs to believe they have a responsibility for the success of the entire organization and an ability to influence the goals and the direction of the organization."

The principal of a senior high school in Indiana, Daniel C. Cilo (personal communication, December 31, 1991), explains his success in these comments.

It is no small task to be dealing with people all day, to be on the firing line and on display all day. It takes stamina. It takes a conviction that this is all worth doing. The principal does influence the school, and the school influences the students, who are our future. What calling could be more vital or rewarding? The principalship is unlike any other position in administration, just as the high school is different from any other organization. Schools are unique organizations and must not compromise their vitality and humanity to fit some abstract, neat, and rational bureaucratic diagram. Where else is there such a rich and splendid pastiche of young people (students) and adults (teachers and staff); those highly trained and those to be taught; and the legitimate exercise of authority by the principal and the need for collegiality by the teachers? It is not enough that each cohabitates peacefully in the same building: the school, also, must educate its students, which is its sacred trust and mission. It would be fatuous for a principal in the 1990s to have less than a missionary zeal about his or her calling as a building leader.

The superintendent of the public schools in Grand Forks, North Dakota, Mark Sanford (personal communication, March 26, 1992), believes the role of the school leader calls for "being a model for others in all that you do, from work habits to visions. Whatever you do is driven by dreams of excellence for your district and its students. You must personalize the success of your district, be willing to live on the cutting edge of change and growth, and display the wisdom and courage necessary to lead your district to the attainment of those dreams."

Dolores A. Ballesteros, superintendent of the Franklin-McKinley School District in California, describes her role as a leader: "I believe in the goodness and inherent qualities and potential of man. Given opportunities and nurturing, man can accomplish way beyond his or her expected potential. Nurturing is best accomplished through positive and intrinsic motivation, multisensory experiences and expansion of one's vision through global opportunities. Children learn best by doing, and knowledge can best be absorbed through opportunities to read, explore, create, and discover."

According to John A. Richman (personal communication, February 28, 1992), a superintendent in New York State:

The key element is "walking your talk," in other words, demonstrating your stated beliefs. I believe that teachers are to be valued. Therefore, I make sure the physical plan is clean, bright, cheery, and safe. I believe in collaborative leadership. Therefore, I strive for "win-win" negotiations, site-based management, peer selection of department chairpersons, and "community" faculty meetings. I believe in proactive transformational leadership skills that emphasize vision and the symbolic and cultural aspects of leadership.

An associate superintendent in a midwestern public school district explained how she works as a school leader.

I act from a set of beliefs that undergird my work as a school administrator: I believe that all persons have innate worth and value as human beings; I believe that all children can learn; I believe that leadership is a participatory process, not a spotlight; I believe that all educators want to be as effective as they can be; I believe we are involved in the most important adventure of all—the growth and development of young people.

From those beliefs, I try to follow a set of practices. I listen more than I speak. I include affected and interested persons in the decision-making process. I expect, encourage, and celebrate different approaches from different administrators to the complex issues of the day. I read widely, and I reflect and review independently and with others. I think out loud a lot, and I try to ask the interesting questions. I act from information and from a sense of what is important. I trust people to mostly do the right thing, and I try to support them in that. I speak clearly and strongly for the needs of children and young people, and I attempt always to make decisions based on what's best for students. And, except for this response, I don't talk much about myself.

The principal of an elementary school in Owens, Wisconsin, Art Feldman (personal communication, February 7, 1992), believes, "A good principal surrounds himself or herself with good people and then helps provide an environment for them to flourish. A person cannot be a leader without having the capacity to provide positive support as the vision moves ever closer to fruition—knowing full well that the vision is forever changing."

An outstanding school leader who serves as the director of curriculum in a school district in Shreveport, Louisiana, Wanda Gunn (personal communication, March 16, 1992), operates as a leader from the following premise:

Surely, all school administrators who achieve any degree of success come to the field of education with a love for children and the basic belief that all children are truly equal and deserve the right to the very best education possible.

If children are to receive this education that is their right, then adults who teach and lead them must be chosen with care and with regard to their own talents and abilities. As a classroom teacher, I saw children who would be affected their entire life by what I said and did. During my service as a principal, I chose with care those persons who would stand before children who would absorb what that teacher taught. As a central office administrator, I still believe in the importance of placing people in positions according to their talents and abilities.

The superintendent of a unified district in California, Cynthia F. Grennan (personal communication, March 5, 1992), expressed the need for strong public education when she said:

I believe that the major investment of this nation must be in young people and that school administrators must take the lead in guaranteeing public educational opportunities for all students.

Education perpetuates a progressive, productive society, an investment for the future. Students, parents, teachers, counselors, and administrators working together must strive to involve business, industry, and the community. We need to teach students all the skills possible for living in our complex global society. And it is our duty to empower our students with positive attitudes and an understanding that learning is a lifelong process.

ROLE MODELS

A number of individuals commented on how they believed school administrators were role models. For example, a principal in Wisconsin said, "Principals are important role models, so as an administrator and building leader, I must set the best possible example to my students and staff. Finally, I believe in allowing school to be a place where learning can be interesting and fun. We need to motivate students to do the best they can do. We work toward developing student potential to its fullest by fulfilling our school motto—'Where everybody is somebody.'"

A high school principal in Ohio felt his role was to "instill in my staff the expectations of excellence as educators and role models while maintaining a sensitivity toward students with problems. I honestly believe education is the most important of all professions. I am proud to be a member of this profession and will continue to strive to provide the best education possible for the kids and community I serve."

A superintendent of schools in Georgia expressed his feelings for the role of school leader when he said:

The ability to communicate and listen while involving others in the decision-making process is vital to maintaining an outstanding school system.

The most important contribution any school superintendent can make is to thoroughly understand his school system, its mission, its philosophy, its objectives, and its learning climate. The ultimate goal is to offer all children the educational opportunities they need to be successful in an ever-changing world.

A middle school principal in Kansas expressed her method of working as a school leader: "I believe in what I do. To lead a team of educators in the teaching of all children under our supervision is an immense challenge. The needs are great. There is so much to do. I can think of no greater mission, and when we are successful, I can think of no greater reward."

SUMMARY

The responses given by the outstanding school leaders in Project Success certainly substantiate their general commitment to American education. Whatever their position in educational administration, the outstanding school administrators cited here understand, acknowledge, and practice their commitment. For them, the interrelationship between the American public educational system and society remains a high priority. These outstanding school administrators have taken seriously their responsibilities in wanting to provide the best possible education for all children.

It has been reported that business is the engine of the U.S. economy. If that is true, the tireless outstanding school leaders in America's schools who give so unselfishly of themselves must be the spark that fires the fuel that feeds the "engine" to keep it running smoothly—the fuel, of course, being education at all levels.

REFERENCES

Barber, B. (1992). *An aristocracy of everyone.* Oxford: Oxford University Press.
Bloom, A. (1987). *The closing of the American mind: How higher education has failed democracy and impoverished the souls of today's students.* New York: Simon and Schuster.
Goodlad, J. I. (1984). *A place called school.* New York: McGraw-Hill.
Johnson, J. A., Collins, H. W., Dupuis, V. L., & Johansen, J. H. (1988). *Introduction to the foundations of American education,* 7th ed. Boston: Allyn and Bacon.
Kimball, R. (1990). *Tenured radicals: How politics has corrupted higher education.* New York: Harper and Row.
Kolwalski, T. J., & Reitzug, U. C. (1993). *Contemporary school administration: An introduction.* White Plains, NY: Longman Publishing Company.
Lane, J. J., & Walberg, H. J. (Eds.). (1987). *Effective school leadership: Policy and process.* Berkeley, CA: McCutchan Publishing Company.
Spring, J. (1991). *American education: An introduction to social and political aspects,* 5th ed. White Plains, NY: Longman Publishing Company.
Sykes, C. (1988). *Profscam: Professors and the demise of higher education.* Washington, DC: Regnery Gateway.

5

COMMITMENT

In the mid-1980s, after the breakup of AT&T, a consultant had the opportunity to work with a company that provided structured interviews to screen employees for several telecommunications companies competing with AT&T. A telephone company in Wisconsin asked the consultant to interview five individuals who had the technical expertise to serve as a controller. Using a structured interview, the assignment was to rank the five candidates according to the highest level of commitment.

Over several days, each candidate interviewed with the chief executive officer. The candidate with the highest commitment was ultimately offered the position. Wisconsin presents a challenge to people who have not been raised in the cold. The CEO wanted the spouse of this finalist to be comfortable with the move north and so invited her to visit Wisconsin to see if she thought she liked the environment enough to tolerate the winters. When she deplaned, it was obvious she was not feeling well. As the day's activities continued, her health began to decline. Later in the day, after being admitted to a local hospital, she died.

You can imagine the confusion! Trying to do his best to accommodate the situation, the CEO indicated he would not hold the finalist to any previous obligations. Knowing the executive had three teenaged daughters in school, the CEO thought it might be better for this candidate to stay in Ohio. To the amazement of the CEO, the executive said, "No, I'm staying here. I made a commitment. My daughters and I are moving to Wisconsin."

Is that what we find in a commitment? Yes. It is an unashamed, full-speed-ahead intention to finish a job no matter what the obstacles.

It is refreshing to study school administrators who, when putting their shoulders to the plow, will not stop until the job is done. People can depend on administrators who are committed. In tough times and good times, knowing that no matter what happens, a person can be counted on to follow through with a commitment creates a tremendous feeling.

Look at the good results when a committed leader sets an example for students. Cleveland Hammonds (personal communication, March 11, 1992), a superintendent in Alabama states:

> If I ignite the fire of dedication, concern, and commitment in others, then I have performed my role as a leader. If you perform your role to find the most able, creative, determined, and dedicated professionals available, then you must as a leader provide the freedom, support, and understanding so they can do their jobs.
>
> Each child contains the potential to fulfill some need that society has. One example is a young high school sophomore who became pregnant. A member of the high school faculty told me she felt that this student, if she could survive this crisis in her life, had a unique surprise for us. The teacher and others provided the support and nurturing for the young mother to finish high school. The surprise was that she went from being an average student to being an honor student. She received a full scholarship at a prestigious private liberal arts college and plans to become a medical doctor.

When administrators make a commitment, they see some intrinsic value in the course of action they have designed for themselves. It is a response to some "mental backbone" that stiffens their resolve to finish what they have begun no matter the hardship. It goes beyond doing this for someone else; it is their mission being addressed, their character on the line, their intentions being played out.

A junior high school principal in South Carolina echoes the sentiments of the previous administrator. One of her imperatives is a belief that everyone makes a difference. She said her school family includes custodial, clerical, and food service staff as well as students, professional staff, and parents. Regardless of the job description, everyone must be committed to the achievement of excellence.

By surrounding herself with people who are genuinely committed to such norms as collegiality, high expectations, honest and open communication, and a caring attitude, she believes, the entire school community cannot help but reap positive results in all areas of its curriculum and in all its programs. Every opportunity for success must be matched with superior efforts by all.

This is an interesting assessment of people's professional obligations to themselves and their students. First, this view recognizes that administrators must contribute their unique talents to the support of students, whether in regard to their nutrition, cleanliness, records, or instruction. Whatever the responsibility required of the adults, it needs to be carried out with an attitude of care and excellence.

A junior high school principal in Missouri recognized the relationship between administrators and teachers in providing good teaching and learning strategies: Personal commitment was the main reason she had been as successful as she was. Her role as principal was not a job to her, so working seventy hours a week came naturally. Further, the success of every child at her school was an equal responsibility shared between her as an administrator and the teachers of her school. Her teachers knew she believed in them and their students, and that she was committed to providing the very best. Her own personal philosophy was grounded in the question "Are we doing the best we can?" If the answer is no, then, she thought, professionals need to be willing to look at what they can do to change and to become better. The response "We've always done it that way" irritated her if used as justification for keeping things at status quo. The challenge, she felt, lay in asking, "Is it the best we can do?"

We hear much about corporations and school districts that are trying to implement total quality management (TQM), a methodology W. Edwards Deming first introduced to industry. Now many companies are committed to implementing it. School administrators who care enough to look at every process in their organizations and to develop improvements are the administrators who will help schools and students succeed in the 21st century.

Professional educators committed to the quality process are constantly looking for ways to improve instructional time for students. They look for ways to cut through the noninstructional activities that decrease the time for quality instruction. Although the schools in the United States generally exceed he number of instructional days of schools of our chief foreign competitors, the amount of time on task for the core subjects in these countries exceeds ours. Thus, a commitment to quality time by administrators also is a requirement for someone wanting to bring about the most profound results.

Gerald Daley (personal communication, February 24, 1992), a superintendent in New Hampshire, stated:

> Success demands total commitment. I know of no successful school administrator who gives less than 100 percent of his or her energy to the job. It is impossible to expect a commitment from others when you are not prepared to give it yourself. Not only should the commitment be total, it should be visible. People need to know that their leaders are willing to give as much of themselves as they expect of others. I try hard to be visible at student plays, concerts, games, or classroom activities to send a message that I care about what our students and their teachers are doing. I am also practicing what I preach—commitment. And it is not without its benefits. One of my biggest rewards as superintendent is to hear how appreciative students, parents, and teachers are that I take the time to attend their activities. They know their superintendent cares.

This superintendent and other administrators have realized that if they are really committed to their students, they will never have a "normal" eight-hour day. The normal day is filled with time and energy commitments that go way beyond the forty-hour week. Yet it is this commitment to the job, the students, and the other professionals that brings into focus the rewards for the long hours.

It is not for external reward that committed administrators devote their energies to their work. An internal mechanism inherent in their commitment establishes its own intrinsic reward. It is the knowledge that they have done everything they can to effect the results they want to see. Having expended time and energy, they have satisfaction in knowing they indeed made a difference that may not have been realized were they not intricately involved in the process. That is the reward. Any outward reward is frosting.

Gerald Freitag (personal communication, March 10, 1992), director of administrative services in Wisconsin, wrote:

> You need to be committed to the task at hand and dedicate your time and talents to achieving the goals of the organization. The job of administrator is not an eight-to-four job. The commitment of time must be in terms of all the time necessary to accomplish the task. All too often, people jealously guard their time and the priority given to their school is lower than it should be.

Cynthia Grennan (personal communication, March 5, 1992), a superintendent in California, feels her effort makes a difference for kids. That is her reward.

> I chose to become a school administrator because I believe I possess the knowledge, expertise, leadership qualities, and commitment to move the schools and district forward to educate young people to assume adult responsibilities in a world yet to be defined. I believe that the major investment of this nation must be in young people and that school administrators must take the lead in guaranteeing public educational opportunities for all students.
>
> I have remained in school administration for two important reasons. First, a variety of local, state, and national evaluative measures indicate I am correct in my belief that I am making a difference for young people. Second, I find the opportunity to build a strong team comprised of students, teachers, counselors, administrators, parents, and community members to be rewarding, both personally and professionally.

A middle school principal in Washington, Susan Galletti (personal communication, February 1, 1992), feels the importance of spending quality time with her students. She exemplifies a characteristic of so many middle school administrators—enjoying being around students. Administrators at the middle level realize how important it is to help support students' efforts to establish their identity, to improve their self-esteem, to recognize peer pressure, to talk incessantly, and to dream the impossible.

> My commitment to students is seen in my visibility with students on a regular basis. I am "out and about" at lunchtime, during breaks, and in classrooms. I still teach when I have an opportunity. Students come to see

me regularly to solve problems. They know I will be receptive to ideas and offer them a course of action to make "good ideas" a reality. Students are very involved in decisions made about the school. They serve on selection committees to hire new staff. They serve on the site-based council. Over half our students are involved in some leadership function (peer clubs, peer tutors, teacher assistants). Most importantly, I am able to "relate" to adolescents, to have fun with them, to have a sense of humor, to understand them.

As a result, they like and respect me. I model this behavior for other adults who act similarly (in their own unique ways) in the school. Students, consequently, work "with" adults in the schoolhouse, not "against" them. Our discipline problems are nearly nonexistent.

We questioned whether an administrator's commitment to spending large amounts of time on the job to ensure quality results decreased with the age of the administrator. We found nothing in our data to indicate any decreases. Those administrators who focused on commitment as their reason for being so successful felt that attribute fit them well when they were younger administrators; now as veterans, they believe it continues to define them well.

Is it equally true that outstanding administrators like kids? Are administrators who like kids outstanding? Our research indicated a resounding yes. The more the administrators felt an affinity with students, the more willing they were to do everything possible to remove any impediments to students' progress. Administrators were willing to take extra time from their own lives to contribute to the growth and development of the students.

A high school principal in Missouri was pleased to be nominated as an outstanding school administrator and mused about why she was selected. She likes kids and supposed that's why some might consider her to be an outstanding administrator. When making school decisions, she has always first tried to determine if what she thinks is best truly is in the best interest of the students. She feels she has an obligation to try to provide the best possible environment in which students can work. Basically, she is honest to a fault and pretty much "tells it like it is." It has worked for her because people do not have to guess where she stands on issues. She thinks an administrator needs to be a role model and stand for something. It is always tougher to take a position than it is to roll over, she believes. Maybe that's the key.

Another Missouri superintendent summed up by indicating that commitment based on a sincere caring has to be a primary factor because success is more than just going through the right motions. A commitment to the success of others and to meeting their needs gives meaning to personal achievement.

For administrators, a commitment to provide a balance between old norms and calculated risks provides side benefits that more than match the degree of the risk incurred or the resistance to the change suggested. A superintendent in Minnesota, wrote to us that when he became superintendent in 1980, his first commitment was to equalize the male and female administrative ratio. Once that was accomplished, new worlds and wonderful possibilities opened to everyone. Equalizing the gender ratio increased their sensitivity with a number of issues and gave the staff a chance to influence the practices and policies of the district. In effect, the pawns became players. An unexpected benefit was the increased civility in their administrative meetings. They became wide-eyed empathetic listeners, anxious to shed the image of sexism. They learned that their actions and language needed to change if they were going to create a partnership where the dignity and worth of each individual was respected. They openly discussed what constituted harassment, sexism, and ignorance on the part of both women and men. Any anger or resentment has washed away with dialogue and time.

The result of equalizing the administrative ratio could not be fully measured; but early on, the trust level in the school system began to improve. Risk taking increased and words like "team" and "partnership" became common as the administrators developed strategies to create a learning environment where all students could be successful. In 1985, in order to focus their energies, a sixty-five-member task force, represented by their school board, administration, staff, and community, was formed to discuss the vision and mission of the district.

Respecting the dignity and worth of each member of the partnership became one of the anchors for their mission. It continues to be the litmus test for all policies and practices in this school district. The inclusion of more women in leadership roles increased the probability that other diversities would be celebrated and included in the educational partnership.

Judith Najib (personal communication, February 24, 1992), an assistant superintendent in Indiana, wrote:

> Whereas people, hard work, and a striving for quality have been essential to my success, I believe the element that has drawn these three values together and contributed most greatly to my success as a school leader has been the ability to recognize and nurture ability in other individuals. As a result, there have been many times in my life when I have found myself surrounded by people of like interest, commitment, dedication, and belief. All these individuals had a vision. Their ability to act helped them to communicate that vision.
>
> We were "like individuals" and persistent in our drive to make schools better places for students. We believed that by making schools better places and teaching students better, we were creating a better future for this country.
>
> Each of us had a vision in our mind of what we could produce by working together. We committed ourselves to that vision and worked with people who began discussions with "if I had my own school" and ended their discussions with "we can do these things here." Our thoughts became action; we put their ability to task and created conditions that were better. Creativity, innovation, ability, and commitment drove better education. As a result, we produced school-within-school concepts, interdisciplinary

bicentennial celebrations, and discussion courses as students were confronted with problems, behaviors, and consequences of behaviors.

Entire school systems became involved in discussions concerning educational beliefs. Because of the talent of identifying ability in others, I have been privileged to participate in "think tank" brainstorming sessions and critiquing events normally reserved for the business or political scene.

John Prasch (personal communication, June 19, 1991), a past superintendent in Nebraska, said he had

a commitment to public education, bordering on missionary zeal, based on my conviction of the importance of preserving the concept of the common school as a unifying power in an ever more pluralistic society. (It is) the only vehicle which insures the economic and social mobility necessary in a democracy, along with the necessity to provide equal access to quality education for all children.

SUMMARY

Outstanding administrators not only displayed a strong commitment to their personal and professional mission but also appreciated the opportunity to work with other professionals who displayed the same level of commitment.

6

INTERPERSONAL RELATIONS

Ask administrators, "What are the sources of your most pleasant and unpleasant experiences?" and they are likely to respond, "People." Administrators depend upon other people in their organizations to carry on day-to-day tasks so that the work is accomplished, goals are met, morale and job satisfaction are high, and all strive to do their best. However, between people in organizations there arise many problems that call for skillful responses and actions by administrators.

SELF-CENTERED ORGANIZATIONS

Imagine what an organization would be like if top- and middle-level administrators thought only of their personal interests, cared not for the needs and concerns of their subordinates, determined that the sole way to achieve goals and to accomplish tasks of the organization was to drive and whip subordinates to produce more and more, and paid little attention to economic and fringe benefits and psychic reward systems for employees. What would working conditions be like for subordinates? What would working conditions be like for administrators? Initially, subordinates might work hard out of fear but then begin to resist. Productivity would decrease, quality of work would drop, errors would creep into the system, morale would sag, and employees might leave the organization. At first, administrators in such an organization might place responsibility for the decline in working conditions upon their subordinates, but as conditions continued to deteriorate, they would themselves pay a heavy price for their oppressive behaviors.

Suppose that top management in an organization such as yours had decided to "get tough," "get more bang for the buck," and "shape everybody up," and after a few weeks of the new approach had noticed a marked decline in productivity, morale, and job satisfaction. What would you do if you were brought into such an organization as a management consultant? Take a few minutes to reflect on what you would do—what information you would want to gather, how you would gather that information, how you would sell your plan to top-level administrators, how you would go about your perceived task, and how you would inform administrators of your findings.

An administrator from Utah (Carlile) described an experience that convinced him of the need to work with people and not to impose one's will upon subordinates.

> The . . . experience . . . came while I was still a classroom teacher. The superintendent of schools asked me to take an assignment that would take me out of the classroom and place me into an eight-school district project. My capacity was to work with a team of individuals composed of the eight districts and provide input from my own school district. This turned into being one of the most profound and interesting experiences that I have had in thirty-four years in education. I found myself in a situation that was not a team effort, but an effort that was totally dominated by the director of the project and her assistant. Both of these individuals were very domineering, very critical of individuals out in the field working with the project, and wanting to have total control of the project's outcome. I think that I learned from this experience all the things that should not be done if I were to ever become an administrator in the public schools. I suppose that reinforces the statement that someone once made, "You can always accomplish some good even if you're serving as a poor example." I feel that I worked in a situation for two years where a poor example of leadership was demonstrated to everyone on the staff. In fact, the situation become so intolerable that I made a request to return to the classroom in the district where I resided. The experiences I had during those two years cemented my belief that the best decisions are made by all who are involved and not just one individual. When I completed my two-year assignment, I was appointed to the position of elementary school principal and was given the opportunity to put into practice my belief that teamwork brings about positive responses.

HEALTHY PEOPLE, HEALTHY ORGANIZATIONS

In healthy organizations, administrators are viewed as capable, fair-minded, perceptive, rational, sensible, and sympathetic individuals. Less capable administrators are often described as autocratic, officious, and dictatorial. How subordinates and others view administrators is a function of how administrators view themselves and how they act. Administrators are hired and given the authority and responsibility to make decisions; to delegate duties to their subordinates; to monitor, supervise, and appraise their subordinates; and to plan, organize, administer, and evaluate numerous programs. Administrators have "the power to make decisions which guide the actions of another" (Simon, 1957, 125). In short, administrators have authority and responsibility to complete tasks, meet goals, and accomplish the mission of the organization.

An elementary school principal from Washington described how to work within the political and power structure in the central office. He advised that one must never "bounce" from one central office administrator to another or try to "go over the head" of an administrator to get a wish fulfilled.

> You must be prepared with a rationale for any request. In most cases this needs to be in writing. Again, the focus of your rationale must be on how it will benefit the students and/or education program. When you present "your case," you must be very proactive and sincere. If you are denied, use "humor" to let the individual and/or committee know you will be back—never, never at this point go over the head of the individual responsible for the decision. As mentioned, know the political/authority structure before you initiate your request. This is the real key to be successful.

AUTHORITY AND POWER

Autocratic, officious, and dictatorial administrators have a perception of their authority, power, and responsibility that permits or even compels them, to boss people around them. Their counterparts, instead, focus upon how to bring out the best qualities of people around them so that all members of the organization, working together, can complete tasks, meet goals, and accomplish the mission of the organization. An example of working together was supplied by Bob Pellegrino (personal communication, April 16, 1992), a middle school principal from Wisconsin.

> [One] example involves an ongoing conflict between a student and a teacher. The student was struggling in many areas at school but seemed to be having a particularly difficult time with a specific teacher. I met with the student and teacher individually and together a number of times with little success. The teacher wanted the student referred for an M-Team for being emotionally disturbed. I refused until we met one more time to develop a contract that had some very specific consequences for inappropriate behavior as well as positive incentives for appropriate behavior. After a few days I checked with the student to see how things were coming. She said, "He's changed. He treats me much nicer." I also checked with the teacher. His response was that she had "really turned it around!" Two months later, they are still doing well.

Would a heavy hand of punishment for the student and blunt directives for the teacher to "bring her into line" have accomplished as much as the principal, teacher, and student working together to resolve differences? Not likely. Equally evident is the influence of the principal in changing the behaviors and attitudes of the student and the teacher. The principal exercised his authority and power to resolve the dispute between the student and teacher by having the parties resolve their differences.

THREE KINDS OF AUTHORITY

Administrators' authority is of three kinds: legal, traditional, and social (i.e., respect for the person or position) (Gorton, 1980). Generally, as long as individuals believe that administrators have the legal power to act, have exercised authority in certain matters over a long period within the organization, or have respect for the administrators or for their positions, they will accept the decisions and actions of administrators. For example, a high school principal who is caring, fair-minded, perceptive, rational, and so on, would not unilaterally change the master schedule from an eight-period day to a four-period one, although he or she would have the legal authority to do so, would have had the responsibility for preparing the master schedule, and could have had the respect of the staff for having designed effective master schedules in the past. To change a master schedule so radically and unilaterally without including staff members in the decision process would suggest an "I'm the boss and that's my job" attitude. The staff's unfavorable reactions to such a decision might come as a complete surprise to an autocratic principal laboring under an "I"-complex.

HIERARCHICAL AND TECHNICAL AUTHORITY

Authority and power are often thought of as synonymous. Complex organizations need to have a hierarchy of authority so that individuals readily agree to work together for the good of the enterprise. Another kind of authority is "technical" in nature; that is, it is authority earned by individuals who have recognized expertise in their field (Newman, 1950).

Again, consider the principal who has technical authority because of recognized expertise for building master schedules. The principal's power to change the master schedule unilaterally may be challenged by staff members. "Power accrues from holding access to or the actual possession of resources—physical, personal, economic, social, or psychological—that someone else desires" (Knezevich, 1975, 45). If staff members are able to overthrow the change, the principal's power is diminished. If staff members perceive, however, that the principal has power to punish them for resisting change, they may meekly go along with a unilateral decision. The authority of the same principal to make such a unilateral decision may go unchallenged because the staff as a group may recognize the principal's legal authority, or legitimacy, to construct a master schedule. Respect for the principal as a person and for the position may also be considered by staff members who protest a unilateral decision to change the master schedule.

TYPES OF POWER

The principal's ability to persuade staff members to accept such a change as being in the best interests of students and staff, curriculum development, resources use, and the like show another aspect of interpersonal relationships. Administrators may use several kinds of power at their disposal: (1) *legitimate*, or the power that is vested in the role or position, (2) *reward*, or the capacity to provide rewards, (3) *coercive*, or the capacity to invoke negative consequences or punishment, (4) *expert*, or the ability or expertise to meet the needs of the unit, and (5) *referent*, or the ability to attract followers (Lunenberg and Ornstein, 1991). Administrators who are able to capitalize upon positive aspects of power are the ones who can influence, persuade, and lead their organizations along the road to success.

Interpretations of Authority and Power

A middle school principal from Massachusetts, Douglas M. Pfeninger (personal communication, March 2, 1992), made a clear distinction about shared decision making in certain circumstances. While he often shared decision making with members of his staff, he expected staff members to defer to his authority when they referred questions to him for his consideration. "I do not, however, use this system (input from assistant principals, cabinet, and entire staff with a vote, if necessary) in all decisions—everything is not shared decisionmaking. The rule of thumb I use is, if you can't accept the answer when you refer a question, don't refer it; answer it yourself."

Administrators who sense a challenge to their authority may lash out at individuals who challenge their right to make decisions or their fairness or in other ways resist administrators' actions and decisions. As tensions heighten between administrators who are beleaguered by subordinates and other individuals or groups, relationships between them may degenerate into staking claims over territory, ill-will on both sides, or win-lose confrontations.

The best position for administrators to take, of course, is to avoid creating devisive conditions that pit administrators or other personnel against staff members, students, parents, patrons, or internal and external groups. Administrators can seek to capitalize upon the authority, responsibility, and power they have to build cooperative, trusting, egalitarian relationships with their colleagues. An elementary school principal from North Carolina defined the principalship as an opportunity to share a vision and not merely as a chance to exert power or command authority.

Education and educational leadership have had long-standing roots in my family. From my grandfather through my father, the role model has been clearly evident: Positive, strong leadership. Leadership for change. Change that clearly reflects the needs of young people. Needs that are not static or, more often than not, easily defined. That is the way of leadership. That is the essence of the principalship. Not a position of power or authority. But an opportunity. To help define. To help refine. It is an opportunity to share a vision and perhaps create a new one based on the visions of the many. The responsibility is awesome. The accountability, inescapable. Leading well means knowing when to follow. How to say no, not always when. Often sacrificing expedience for listening one more time. Leading well means being there and sometimes not. And knowing the difference.

This administrator had developed a view of the principalship directed toward positive action, change, the future, and reflective leadership.

Meeting Others' Needs

Individuals' needs can be categorized by (1) need satisfaction, that is, physical and security needs, social needs, and egoistic needs; or (2) means of satisfaction, whether intrinsic or through the job, around the job or the work environment, or off the job (Strauss and Sayles, 1972). Administrators can play upon or enhance individuals' needs, for example, by threatening job dismissal to those in fear of job security, by letting persons volunteer for assignments that are ego satisfying, or by making working conditions on the job as pleasant as possible. The interrelationships between need satisfaction and means of satisfaction are complex, and administrators can inventively determine how to meet other people's needs, as a middle school principal from Massachusetts noted. The metaphor of weaving is used to suggest the intricate relationship among support staff, students, mission, climate, involvement, risk taking, policies, and implementation and support.

An outstanding administrator weaves everyone into the fabric, including support staff. He stimulates a sense of mission on behalf of kids. He works to truly empower everyone and is able to create a climate where involvement and risk taking are the norm. The staff learns how to unction as a group and policies, practices, etc., are implemented with strong support.

Satisfying needs on the job. Needs for compensation, security, and advancement are so basic they cannot be overlooked. Disputes over salary or wage inequities, fear of new technologies or the loss of positions due to declining enrollments, and thwarted ambitions can produce cancerous conditions within organizations. Administrators must examine what they can do to reduce salary or wage inequities, eliminate fear of new technologies or reduction-in-force, and provide ways for individuals to achieve more responsible jobs or obtain promotions. The benefits of engaging staff members in decisions affecting their job assignments were related by a superintendent from Minnesota. She concluded that decisions made by teachers about reassignments of the teaching staff in one instance were better than ones she could have made by herself.

> Recently we had to decide on the teaching assignments for our elementary teaching staff for next year. I had a team of six teachers working with me on this most difficult task. We debated the best assignments and configurations but finally decided to open the options up to the entire staff. Everyone could say what they personally wanted. Although we could not guarantee any choices, we did our best to honor requests. However, we finally came down to a series of assignments that we simply could not honor. The teachers were then empowered by me to go to their fellow teachers and "work out a solution." In this process, there was give and take and there was compromise. In the final analysis I ended up with many more different assignments than I would have given out had I done the entire exercise behind my closed door. Also, I ended up with a very happy staff, which I doubt I would have had if I had been the sole decision maker on this exercise.

Satisfying social needs. Well-adjusted individuals desire companionship, friendship, and identification with formal and informal groups. By establishing teamwork and other collaborative relationships, administrators can enable individuals to help others, be helped by others, garner a sense of cooperation, and build esprit de corps. Healthy relationships also depend upon treating persons fairly, giving recognition for accomplishments, giving individual feedback, and paying attention to people. In the latter case, some individuals consume the attention of others around them, whereas others may work well without much attention. "Teachers value accurate, useful, consistent, and constructive feedback from their principals. They want to know how well they are performing their jobs. The more principals help them understand that, the more satisfied [they are] on the job" (Whaley, 1994, 47). Such feedback improves teachers' job skills, satisfies teachers' need to be valued members of a school's staff, raises the perception of principals' instruction leadership, and cements a bond between teachers and their principals. An elementary school principal from Michigan, Karin Falkenstein (personal communication, April 13, 1992), enumerated several methods she used to give staff members and students feedback about their accomplishments.

> I keep a file noting workshops, seminars, classes, and so on, taken by each teacher that also indicates areas of special interest. Often teachers will investigate areas of personal interest and can then become a staff expert in that area. For example, a teacher with a hyperactive son or daughter investigating A.D.D. helps him or her and the school staff. All training is reported on summative teaching evaluations each year so that credit is always given for efforts even if there are no financial rewards to teachers. I send a personal handwritten note to every child every year

regarding school efforts based on report cards, conversations with teachers, my observations, and so on. I've sent letters to spouses and parents of staff members thanking them for their support of extra time spent outside of school by their family member. Besides personal notes of support, I send formal letters with copies to the superintendent and personnel file for staff efforts. Every staff member is included in these pats on the back.

From her records of teachers' participation in growth activities, Karin Falkenstein was able to provide them with recognition of their accomplishments and had sources of expertise to call upon to meet specific needs in her school.

Satisfying egoistic needs. Individuals can gain a sense of achievement by having others recognize the importance of their work, how their work fits into the overall mission and goals of the organization, their skill, their progress and development, their productivity, and their ingenuity and imagination. How can administrators meet physical, security, social, and egoistic needs? Art Feldman (personal communication, February 7, 1992), an elementary school principal from Wisconsin, noted how "little things" are really important matters.

A school is a people-intensive organization. Establishing and maintaining good relationships with staff and students is crucial if one is to be effective. Little things are important, like being visible, remembering birthdays, letting folks know about the good things you observe, and always allowing for input from students and staff as decisions that affect them are made. Our school has a student "Action" club that allows students the opportunity to have ownership in the school. We also have a School Effectiveness Team that allows for staff input in the decision-making process. This is a team, made up of teachers, educational assistants, and support personnel, helps chart the direction the school must go to provide quality education for our students. We are talking about "best practice" in every classroom. We think the challenge is clear. Too often, past practice continues far too long after we know it is ineffective.

Other factors also play upon interpersonal relationships. McClelland (1961) proposed that employees had three positive needs: achievement, power (control over people), and affiliation (acceptance by others); they also had a negative need: avoidance of failure. Thus three individuals may have three different purposes for accepting an assignment; one to accomplish a goal, another to get control of the group or gain influence over the group's work, and a third to gain enjoyment from working with others in the group. A fourth individual may not join the group because of fear of being unable to contribute anything to the group.

Other psychological factors bear upon need satisfaction. For example, some individuals will work for less pay in a role perceived to be prestigious than in a role that may pay more but carry less prestige, for example, sanitation worker. Others will avoid some roles and be satisfied with less pay, power, and responsibility. At a small, private college, Charley was offered the opportunity to be head custodian of one building with another custodian reporting to him. After much mental turmoil, Charley declined the opportunity because the responsibility for supervising one other custodian was more than he wanted. An elementary school principal from Kentucky, Charles Edwards (personal communication, February 10, 1992), noted that recognition, commitment, and willingness to work were important factors in achieving goals.

Sharing recognition with everyone, and we have had a lot, is the only way to achieve something for which recognition is deserved. No matter how hard you work, a school cannot change and be successful unless everyone is committed and willing to work. People will do this if they receive their share of professional and personal recognition.

JOB SATISFACTION

Job satisfaction for administrators and subordinates in organizations such as schools is a measure of how ready people are to work to achieve the organization's objectives. Job satisfaction is also a goal through which individuals' needs can be met. Because one's job is such an important part of life, jobs should be made as satisfying as possible. Administrators can seek to determine physical, psychological, social, and economic conditions that enhance job satisfaction. A superintendent from Iowa stressed the importance of the human element to attainment of the school's mission: "Emphasize the importance of the human element. The most important decisions made relate to whom we attract to the district. If the district attracts talent, helps the people grow, and assists everyone to work focused on a common mission, then the district will serve its clientele effectively."

Many factors can lead to job satisfaction. Consider various positions under your supervision and reflect how the following may be related to job satisfaction for those positions: accomplishment, autonomy, identification, job enlargement, job enrichment, job rotation, knowledge required, mental effort required, movement, nature of the work, pace, physical conditions, physical effort required, opportunity for social interaction, required skills, stress, and variety. Can some positions be made more satisfying by providing more autonomy, job enrichment, and variety? Perhaps others can be improved by providing training to meet skills required for the job or for new skills that must be acquired to meet job enlargement. Successful administrators look for and find ways to increase job satisfaction among new hires and veterans, unskilled and skilled, self-motivated and unmotivated, and those happy in their work and those who are not.

TEAMWORK

Although persons may seemingly work alone for much of the day, their work is shaped by their co-workers; consequently, persons behave as members of a group.

The norms and influences of groups may have more influence over personnel than do administrators, who must understand why and how groups form and act to interpret the web of interactions around them. A group may assign a member a much greater identity than would an administrator. Further, any enjoyment, pleasure, suffering, or wrong experienced by a member of the group is shared by fellow members. Administrators' actions upon one individual may, therefore, affect more than one person in an organization.

Some tips on how to develop a team spirit were provided by Harlan Else (personal communication, February 13, 1992), a superintendent from Colorado. Note that he reported spending a good portion of his time inculcating esprit de corps in his staff.

> I spend a significant amount of time (25-30 percent) in building a sense of cohesiveness and collegiality among and between the many various groups in our organization and the community. I am a good listener. As one person described me, I listen with my skin. I try to understand the feelings, values, and ideas expressed by individuals and groups when I am meeting with them.

People join groups for sources of assistance, friendship, identity, and protection and may build ties with one or more groups that transcend loyalty to a role, position, or organization. Groups form, dissolve, reform, and merge with other groups that in turn change individuals' relationships with their co-workers. Individuals may become caught between conflicting elements of two groups and be forced to be loyal to one at the expense of the other.

Groups also form on the basis of work location. Individuals who work together at one end of the building, in a pod or team, are more likely to form relationships among themselves rather than among individuals who work more distant from each other. Soon a group takes on the characteristics of the parent organization and has its identity, leaders, goals, rules and norms, privileges, status symbols, and values. Any of a group's characteristics may lead its members to support or oppose the organization's purposes and goals. A high school principal from Illinois commented that her success as a school administrator could be attributed to human relations skills.

> If I had to select one specific reason why I am perceived as an outstanding school administrator, it would have to be the ability to interact with people in a way that allows for tasks to be accomplished and at the same time maintain staff morale and support individual self-worth. I value my human relations skills. They are my strongest asset. People who work with me describe me as decisive, open, supportive, and caring about the welfare of students and staff. I try to treat my staff as I would want them to treat students. I hold loyalty in high regard but believe that loyalty must be earned, not demanded. Ethics and integrity are far more important.

A group's cohesiveness greatly determines the extent to which a group's members will accept standards imposed by the group and whether they will act in unison against perceived threats from other groups, administrators, or even the group's own members. In a highly cohesive group, a newcomer may be unwelcome at first and may even want to leave after a few days or weeks on the job. Groups small in size are homogeneous, have high status, are isolated from other groups, have in the past had success in defending themselves, and can communicate easily, and are likely to be highly cohesive. The lesson for administrators is that they must be acutely aware of how their actions may be received by a highly cohesive group. Thus, hiring a new staff member to fit in with such a group has obvious implications for the degree of participation by the group in the recruitment, selection, assignment, and induction of a new member. Identification with and loyalty to a group cannot be overlooked by administrators as they contemplate decisions that may affect one or more members of the group.

Administrators in schools with strong unions need to bear in mind collective bargaining agreements in effect that may limit class size and other working conditions. Any decisions that may violate a clause in an agreement, even one that is pro-student, may be met with opposition from members of a larger group—the teachers union. Informal conversations with members of the teachers association or other union can serve as a channel of communication that can prevent problems from arising. Such informal conversations can reveal diverse points of view, identify sources of discontent, and prevent the filing of grievances.

The importance of the administrative team was reinforced by Bonnie Ferrier (personal communication, February 3, 1992), an elementary school principal from Maryland: "Our administrative team is a model of collaborative efforts to foster school improvement. Tasks are delegated to assistant principals, clerical staff, team leaders, and resource teacher in order to prohibit management duties from interfering with the principal's visibility and active involvement in other areas of the school's operation."

MOTIVATION

One of the expectations of good interpersonal relations among administrators and staff members is that motivation to work will be increased because of good rapport, amity, and harmony within the organization. The complexity of interpersonal relationships among individuals of differing personalities and needs, dynamics among groups of different composition and requirements, administrators' styles and skills, vertical and lateral communication patterns, and other variables is no guarantee that even though equanimity exists within the organization, motivation will be high. William Ecker (personal communication, April 28, 1992), a superintendent from Maryland, emphasized the importance of integrity and interpersonal skills as basic to the success of administrators: "I believe an outstanding school administrator needs two basic attributes: (1) integrity and

(2) positive human relations skills, which require good listening skills and a sincere interest in others."

The job of administrators—to get their work done through other people—requires them to be highly skilled in motivating their subordinates to work on assigned tasks as well as on nonduty ones. At times their job also requires them to be able to motivate students, volunteers, and parents, for example, to work on committees, projects, and other school-related activities.

Approaches to Motivation

What ways of motivating persons do you find to be effective? Do you have a few rules of thumb that you follow? Where and how did you learn motivational methods?

All leaders must develop a basic understanding of personnel motivation, recognizing its complexity and theoretical foundations. Individuals will respond differently to motivational strategies based upon their experiences, the work environment, and the situation. Administrators must take these factors into consideration when seeking to motivate faculty members. Having the ability to understand the distinction between satisfaction and motivation is also critical. (Lehman, 1989, 79-80)

Can you readily identify individuals who can inspire people to do their best work for lengthy periods, even under trying conditions? What qualities do these individuals have in common? How do they treat people they supervise? How do they distribute rewards? Compare your observations about such individuals to the following suggestions.

Be the boss. Those who rely upon the principle of authority believe the way to motivate others is to exert themselves with threats, bullying, and sanctions. Such an approach will have little effect upon teachers with tenure; employees with strong linkages to groups and unions who will offer them protection; those who have learned that their value in the organization comes from their ability to think as much, if not more, than their ability to follow orders; and those who have good records of past productivity.

A common practice is to set goals so high that they cannot be reached, to raise goals higher and higher, and to keep pressure on employees so that they work at full capacity. Administrators may themselves be under such pressure and be tempted to use the same tactics on their subordinates. The application of continuous pressure may suffice in the short run but will probably be counter-productive in the long run. Most persons work well under some pressure, particularly with simple tasks; however, determining the lines between some, enough, and too much pressure is difficult, especially if work requires creativity. Placing people under too much pressure will result in acts of aggression, frustration, game playing, incentive to work to the minimum to avoid punishment, job dissatisfaction, lowered morale, lowered productivity, banding together to form opposition, poor health and psychosomatic illnesses, and other negative reactions.

Be benevolent. Competitive compensation packages, attractive fringe benefits, liberal leave policies, low workloads, employee assistance programs, low-key supervisory practices, and other features of good working conditions exemplify the benevolent approach. Those who adhere to this approach believe that employees will work hard out of appreciation for good working conditions, loyalty to their benefactors, or job satisfaction. In schools, where many employees have graduate degrees in addition to college degrees, the notion that employees will work harder and longer out of gratitude will not last long. Employees whose basic economic needs are met may resent "gifts" that are bestowed upon them, come to expect more and more gifts, or perceive that "gifts" may be taken away if their work displeases top management. An assistant superintendent for school relations in Kentucky wrote about how she translated her understanding of employees' needs into sensitive actions.

> I am a good listener who cares about people. I have treated my staff and the principals I have supervised as individuals with real problems and concerns that deserve my understanding. They know they can come to me for advice or bring their ideas and receive a sympathetic audience. I support others and make a point of being sure they get credit for their ideas and good work.

Administrators who believe that increased productivity follows high morale ignore a significant factor. If all persons enjoy benefits, the reward system may ignore quality work itself and offer no incentive to increase quality and productivity. Instead, top-level administrators should spend their efforts in making jobs more rewarding instead of tinkering with reward systems.

Be friends. Administrators who follow this principle believe they can get something, if not the most, out of subordinates by compromises with them on extra duties, planning time, use of resources, absence and leave policies, and other job and work factors. Thus principals may look the other way when teachers arrive late, knowing they will take home papers to grade or perform other school duties after hours or over the weekend. This approach limits administrators' efforts to increase quality or quantity of work and to introduce changes and innovations into the school.

Be competitive. Everybody likes to be a winner! "Pay increases and promotions should go to those who do the best work" is an adage of those who believe in competition as a motivating force. That employees who win the promotion or merit increase also receive a sense of achievement, self-improvement, and status is a similar tenet. Where seniority is a factor, however, competition does little more than render resentment among employees. Also, competition may work best among groups where the sense of individual contribution or failure is lessened. But competition does not seem to motivate persons who disparage the "dog-eat-dog" approach or those who dislike competition. The measurement of who is more successful is difficult and may turn subordinates into being overly dependent for recognition of achievement by their superordinates. Such an attitude may pervade an entire organization so that all persons become intent on pleasing immediate supervisors. One loss, of course, is that supervisors look away from their responsibilities and instead attend to gaining favor from their immediate supervisors. With the low ratio of administrators to staff members in school and the fixed salary schedule, competition offers few promotions and merit increases; thus not everyone can be a winner. Before installing a motivation system based on competition, administrators should weigh carefully the benefits and drawbacks from such an approach.

Be self-motivated. Capitalizing upon people's internal motivation focuses upon letting employees gain satisfaction from doing their jobs well. In this approach, administrators believe that persons find enjoyment in their jobs and rely little upon motivators based on extrinsic factors. McGregor's Theory Y complements an approach that focuses upon the willingness of employees to attain organizational objectives. The concepts of participatory management, site-based management, and collaboration are based upon the principle that employees gain or earn satisfaction from the achievement, accomplishments, and ownership in matters relating to their work, status, and self-esteem. A secondary school principal from New York wrote that a major reason for his success could be attributed to the collaborative working relationship he had with people in his school: "The second reason for my success is the working relationship I have with the faculty and student body. I work collaboratively with the faculty on all issues that affect their lives. We work together to solve problems, raise standards and expectations, and strive for excellence. The same is true with students. There is great mutual respect and trust."

Self-motivation works well in organizations (1) where organizational goals fit well with employees' goals, that is, in schools where learning is a shared goal; (2) that provide employees a high degree of autonomy, as in schools where teachers and other employees work with loose supervision; and (3) where basic physical and security needs are met. Vroom's (1964) concept of paths-goals analysis posits that employees will be motivated if they perceive that efforts on their part will lead to one or more goals that they value or will meet their needs. Other factors, such as feedback about performance, reward that matches personal needs or fair and equitable rewards, the perceived results of harder or more work, and attention to egoistic needs will influence the degree to which elf-motivation may be used.

Be my delegate. Another approach to motivate employees is delegation. Career ladders, job enrichment, and job enlargement offer opportunities for administrators to delegate work and to restructure positions so that individuals have more autonomy, some supervisory duties, and a broader picture of their importance to the school.

Because most administrators have more work than they can accomplish, the concept of delegation can be used to the advantage of both administrator and supervisees. Knowing which supervisee has the skills to perform a task or function, phrasing the task or function to be performed, and applying a degree of supervision are important aspects of delegation. If a supervisee is asked to perform a task without the skills, if the task is phrased so explicitly that the supervisee can exercise no initiative, and if the administrator continually monitors the performance of the delegate, then soon the word will spread: Delegation means "I was set up to fail," "It took longer to hear what to do than to do it," and "I never had a minute's peace after I agreed to do it."

Be clear. Subordinates want to know what is expected of them. Administrators can improve interpersonal relationships by establishing clear goals, being fair and consistent, enforcing rules fairly and impersonally, assigning specific roles and responsibilities, clarifying supervisory relationships, and providing orientation and induction programs.

Successful administrators also realize that their administrative work is different from that of their subordinates and neither try to do their subordinates' jobs nor provide such close supervision that subordinates feel spied upon constantly. Focusing upon long-range issues and strategic plans, upon staff development and inservice training, is desirable, as is enhancing communication. However, the kind and degree of supervision subordinates want may vary from culture to culture, by preparation and background, and by personal preferences.

Be decisive. Administrators must make decisions, as Harry Truman so succinctly noted, because the buck stops on their desks. Yet administrators can create a healthy climate and minimize negative factors without being dictatorial. How supervisors act toward their supervisees creates a climate of trust, distinguishes between specific and nonspecific praise, and enhances a feeling of loyalty. Administrators seen as approachable, interested in personal concerns, willing to talk about items of interest to subordinates, and showing consistent patterns over a long period will develop good rapport. Subordinates want to be consulted about matters that concern them directly, to have their suggestions given a fair hearing, to receive fair treatment, to be permitted to make mistakes and to learn from them, and to receive training so that they can improve their knowledge and skills. Although administrators must make decisions, sometimes ones that are unpopular, the decisions need not be made in a vacuum nor without attending to the needs of the organization and of employees.

Be a team builder. Most individuals gravitate to groups for identification, recognition, and support, and the desire for membership in groups can be used to achieve organizational and unit goals. Team members can also gain social satisfaction, be more productive, enhance communication among themselves, and feel empowered (Kanpol, 1990, 104). In the process they support organizational goals, norms, and standards. On the negative side, teams can become so closely knit that they reject outsiders, protect their members from any external changes, and otherwise resist efforts for the greater good.

Teams can be built and enhanced by considering several variables such as putting friends together, avoiding the creation of competing groups, providing training on how to work together or how to include everyone in the team, rewarding all members of a group, introducing new members by using a mentoring or buddy system, and setting up conditions so that teamwork pays off for everyone. Not all teams will function well together, and administrators must find ways of improving relationships within a team or restructuring the team. Administrators will need to monitor the performance of teams as well as the performance of individuals. Setting up a team—by directive or by seeking volunteers—is merely the first step in building a team. Teams can be allowed to set their own goals, rules, time for meeting, time for meeting with a supervisor, and the like. Administrators can meet with teams to gather information on their progress, provide information, pose issues, seek consensus, and engage in varied forms of decision making. The team approach has brought good results to an elementary school principal from Arizona.

> I think the reason I am able to get good results in my school is that I use a team approach and try to work "through people" to get the job done. I try to convey through both my words and my actions that each person in the school, from custodian to teacher to cafeteria server, has an important role in the whole picture and that the "team" does not function without each piece of the puzzle. I try to build a positive, supportive atmosphere where each person feels safe to take a risk and to go out a the limb a little if need be. Without risk, we do not grow and learn.

Successful administrators use the "we" approach rather than the "I" approach in their schools. By working together as a team, administrators and their staff members build each other up, establish a healthy working environment, encourage risk taking, grow and learn, and strive to accomplish the mission of the school. Administrators can energize individuals and teams to perform at high levels by understanding how to use varied motivators.

WORKING WITH GROUPS

Administrators work with staff members, students, parents and guardians, patrons, business and community leaders, and other individuals in formal and informal settings, both individually and in groups. In school systems, many important issues are discussed and decisions are made in large as well as small groups. Administrators who understand how individuals work in groups are able to capitalize upon the leadership opportunities that groups provide. For example, an issue may be discussed by individuals throughout a unit, often with administrators seeking out persons for face-to-face discussions, but it may eventually be settled by a large group. Thus, for instance, a discussion to introduce authentic forms of assessment may be bandied about in classrooms, hallways, lounges, and offices but may be formally adopted at a meeting of the faculty. Astute administrators may have laid elaborate groundwork for such a change but would be well advised to undertake equally elaborate planning for the faculty meeting where a decision will be made. Careful planning of the agenda, such as provisions for reports on the topic and a question-and-answer period, could lead to an open discussion of the topic and a decision acceptable to most, if not all, of the faculty.

Leaders of Groups

Groups and teams have their informal leaders, particularly in the absence of formal leaders. Administrators can cultivate the advice, cooperation, and insight of informal leaders to enhance relationships within teams and with organizational goals. The roles other individuals take in groups or teams can be studied and inservice training can be provided to increase skills in group and teamwork. By careful observation in meetings and other settings, administrators can learn much about how individuals perform in a group.

Susan Galletti (personal communication, February 1, 1992), a middle school principal from Washington, uses group process skills to increase participation of staff members, students, and parents in decision making.

I use a variety of group process skills, including jigsaw, fishbowl, prioritization exercises, consensus exercises, and active listening and paraphrasing. Group process, site-based decision making, and authentic involvement of parents, students, and staff are the "way we do business." This includes being involved fully in budget, scheduling, and hiring practices.

Roles in Groups

Some roles that persons frequently take in a group include the following ones (Benne and Sheats, 1948).

1. Initiator. Proposes new ideas, goals, procedures, methods, solutions.
2. Information Seeker. Asks for facts, clarification, or information from other members, or suggests information is needed before making decisions.
3. Information Giver. Offers facts and information, personal experiences, and evidence that is useful to accomplishing the task.
4. Opinion Seeker. Draws out convictions and opinions of others, asks for clarification of position or values displayed.
5. Opinion Giver. States own belief or opinion, expresses a judgment.
6. Clarifier. Elaborates on ideas expressed by another, often by giving an example, illustration, or explanation.
7. Coordinator. Clarifies relationships among facts, ideas, and suggestions or suggests an integration of ideas and activities of two or more members.
8. Orienter. Clarifies purpose or goal, defines position of the group, summarizes or suggests the direction of the discussion.
9. Energizer. Prods group to greater activity or to a decision, stimulates activity, or warns of need to act while still time.

10. Procedure Developer. Offers suggestions for accomplishing ideas of others or handles such tasks as seating arrangements, operating equipment, or passing out papers.
11. Recorder. Keeps written record on paper, chart, or chalkboard, serving as group's memory.

Administrators can enhance their effectiveness in groups, whether they are in charge or not, by being alert to the roles others play and by being aware of roles they themselves may take, for example, that of information giver, supplying vital information at a critical time in a discussion.

Team-Centered Roles

Some behaviors establish and maintain cooperative interpersonal relationships and a group- or team-centered orientation. Among these are the following four:

1. Supporter. Praises, agrees, indicates warmth and solidarity with others or goes along with them.
2. Harmonizer. Mediates differences between others, reconciles disagreement, conciliates.
3. Tension Reliever. Jokes or brings out humor in a situation, reduces formality and status differences, relaxes others.
4. Gatekeeper. Opens channels of communication, brings in members who otherwise might not speak, sees that all have equitable chance to be heard.

Likewise, administrators may look for persons who are supporters of good ideas or may serve themselves as supporters of ideas that appeal to them as groups are processing their assignments. One's ability to persuade others is not limited to the act of initiating ideas but includes supporting the ideas of others and filling essential roles at key intervals.

Self-Centered Roles

Self-centered roles consist of behaviors that satisfy only individual needs and do not serve the group or team. Most self-centered roles are a detriment to accomplishing the task of a group or team. Some of the harmful self-centered roles are included in the following list.

1. Blocker. Constantly raises objections, insists nothing can be done, or repeatedly brings up the same topic after the rest of the group has disposed of it.

2. Aggressor. Deflates status of others, expresses disapproval, jokes at expense of another member, expresses ill will or envy.
3. Recognition Seeker. Boasts, calls attention to self, relates irrelevant personal experiences, seeks sympathy or pity.
4. Confessor. Uses group as audience for his or her mistakes, feelings, and beliefs irrelevant to the group task, or engages in personal catharsis.
5. Playboy. Displays a lack of participation in group task by making jokes and cynical comments, and through horseplay and ridicule.
6. Dominator. Tries to run the group by giving directions, ordering, flattering, interrupting, and insisting on his or her own way.
7. Special Interest Pleader. Speaks up primarily for the interests of a different group, acting as its representative, apologist, or advocate.

Familiarity with self-centered roles is also useful to administrators. By quickly recognizing the potential damage self-centered individuals can inflict on the work of the group, administrators may interject ideas that steer the group in a positive direction. Only a few words may be needed to leapfrog the objections of a blocker or deflate a dominator if made by an administrator who is decisive and sensitive to the needs of the group.

Feedback

Administrators can learn much about others, and themselves, by observing the behaviors of others and themselves in groups and teams, in both formal and informal settings. Information obtained from such observations should be shared so that members can become better group or team players. Feedback is a way of helping others to consider changing their behaviors. Feedback communicates to one or all members of a group or team how they affect others. Feedback helps an individual to keep behaviors on target and thus helps the group or team to accomplish its task.

Some criteria for useful feedback include the following:

1. It is descriptive rather than evaluative. As a description of the evaluator's own reaction, such feedback leaves the evaluee free to use it as seen fit. Avoiding evaluation language reduces the need for an individual to react defensively.
2. It is specific rather than general. To be told that one is a dominator will probably not be as useful as to be told, "When we were deciding the issue, you did not listen to what others said, and I felt forced to accept your arguments or be attacked by you as you attacked Jane and John."
3. It takes into account the needs of both the receiver and giver of feedback. Feedback can be destructive when it serves only the giver's

needs and fails to consider the needs of the person on the receiving end.

4. It is directed toward behavior the receiver can do something about. Frustration is only increased when a person is reminded of some shortcoming over which he or she has no control.

5. It is solicited rather than imposed. Feedback is most useful when the receiver has formulated the kind of question that those observing can answer.

6. It is well timed. In general, feedback is most useful at the earliest opportunity after the given behavior, depending, of course, on the person's readiness to hear it, the support received from others, and so on.

7. It is checked to ensure clear communication. One way of doing this is to have the receiver rephrase the feedback to confirm the sender's message.

8. When feedback is given in a training group, both giver and receiver have the opportunity to check the accuracy of the feedback with others in the group.

Feedback, then, is a way of giving help. It is a corrective mechanism for individuals who want to learn how well their behavior matches their intentions, and it is a must for establishing one's identity. The principles of feedback apply as well in other circumstances, such as in formal and informal classroom observations. Effective administrators are alert to opportunities to observe their subordinates in action, to note specific behaviors they have observed, to discover talents that may previously have seemed hidden (Black, 1994), to give direct feedback about those specific behaviors, and to focus attention upon successful accomplishment of a task or goal.

The power of the group over a single person, even someone at the apex of the leadership pyramid, was related by a superintendent from Oregon.

I remember clearly one time when a veteran teacher responded to me with the comment, "Young man, I have seen a lot just like you come and go." This reality check is a reminder of the leadership requirement to understand some basics of group process in bringing about change. My comments about doing things "with" rather than "to" people goes back to this story. Lasting, effective, and systematic change does not "trickle down" or otherwise happen from the top. Leaders must lead, but lead through creation of stakeholders and ownership in the process.

Administrators must work cooperatively with groups to be successful. In many instances, administrators join units that have entrenched groups with powerful influences over members of the school community. The task confronting administrators in such instances, then, is to learn how to work with and through individuals and groups for the common good.

SUMMARY

Administrators set the tone for interpersonal relationships within their organizations. They must be able to establish and maintain positive working relationships with members of their staff and their school's community. In addition to providing good models of rapport, administrators can foster positive interpersonal relationships by setting high expectations for others, developing plans for building good relationships among their staff members, and following through with actions that elevate esprit de corps in their units. One factor that influences the kind of relationships is the way administrators use their authority, influence, and power. Successful administrators use their positions as opportunities for enhancing the work of others, recognizing the efforts of their staff members, and motivating them to continue their productive efforts as individuals and as members of work groups, task forces, teams, and committees. Because so much is accomplished through group efforts, administrators need to know how to garner the benefits of individuals working together and to use their knowledge of group processes to increase the benefits of human resources.

REFERENCES

Benne, K. D., & Sheats, P. (1948). Functional roles of group members. *Journal of Social Issues, 4*, 41-49.

Black, S. (1994, January). Different kinds of smart. *The Executive Educator, 16*(1), 24-27.

Gorton, R. A. (1980). *School administration and supervision: Important issues, concepts, and case studies* (2nd ed.). Dubuque, IA: Wm. C. Brown Company Publishers.

Kanpol, B. (1990). Empowerment: The institutional and cultural aspects for teachers and principals. *NASSP Bulletin, 74*(528), 104-107.

Knezevich, S. J. (1975). *Administration of public education* (3rd ed.). New York: Harper & Row.

Lehman, L. E. (1989, November). Practical motivational strategies for teacher performance and growth. *NASSP Bulletin, 73*(520), 76-81.

Lunenberg, F. C., & Ornstein, A. C. (1991). *Educational administration: Concepts and practices*. Belmont, CA: Wadsworth Publishing Company.

McClelland, D. C. (1961). *The achieving society*. Princeton, NJ: Van Nostrand.

Newman, W. H. (1950). *Administrative action*. Englewood Cliffs, NJ: Prentice-Hall.

Simon, H. A. (1957). *Administrative behavior* (2nd ed.). New York: Macmillan.

Strauss, G., & Sayles, L. R. (1972). *Personnel: The human problems of management* (3rd ed.). Englewood Cliffs, NJ: Prentice-Hall.

Vroom, V. H. (1964). *Work and motivation*. New York: Wiley.

Whaley, K. W. (1994). Leadership and teacher job satisfaction. *NASSP Bulletin, 78*(564), 47-50.

7

INNOVATION AND
QUALITY

Are students, staff members, parents, patrons, and school board members in your community calling for change of some fundamental way of conducting schooling, a procedure, or a program? Pressures for change, innovative ways of allocating resources, more cost-effective controls, new programs or, conversely, a return to the so-called basics, and similar demands weigh heavily upon administrators. Many of the demands for change, improvement, and innovation, as well as resistance to change, fall upon administrators, and they are the ones called upon to answer why test scores are low, why tax increases have risen faster than the rate of inflation, why a new literacy program omits phonics, or some other why.

THE ROLE OF ADMINISTRATORS

Administrators are faced with acknowledging that the status quo is good but could be improved and with promoting the concept that improvement is not likely to come without change. Further, unless a change is made, an improvement cannot be noted in comparison with the status quo. Finally, a change can bring about a greater understanding of and appreciation for the status quo, for the change itself and improvement from the change, and for others' effects of change (Costello, 1993). The search for excellence, improvement, quality, and continuous refinement cannot be abandoned if administrators are to perform a basic function of their positions (Jablonski, 1991; Bonstingl, 1992; Neuroth, Plastrik, and Cleveland, 1992). An elementary school principal in Hawaii has her guiding principles clearly in mind. "Belief in productivity and satisfaction in the school guide what I do as an administrator. I believe in continued school improvement done hand in hand with good human relations skills. What I do is based on my philosophy of having high goals and expectations and achieving these by collaborating with all involved."

Fostering Change

Much of administrators' successes depend upon their ability to maintain honor and respect for the status quo and to create and foster a desire for change that leads to improvement in learning and other aspects of education (Schaaf, 1991). A high school principal from Kansas noted the primary reason for his success: "First, I am willing to continue to learn and grow as a professional. I have not found a single technique or program that will cure all our problems. Therefore, I am open to all ideas that will help me develop a variety of solutions to our problems. This means I read all I can and pick my colleagues' brains as much as I can."

Enlisting Support

Even more of administrators' successes depend upon the cooperation, enthusiasm, and support from others, particularly when change is desired and improvement is sought. Resistance to change by one or more individuals most affected by change can retard, sidetrack, or even prevent a change from being implemented. Consequently, administrators must be as knowledgeable about and skilled in the installation of change, or the change process, as they are in the nature of the innovation itself (Senge, 1993). For example, administrators who see a need for change to a whole-language program or for outcome-based education must battle on two fronts: convincing people of the worthiness of the change and training staff to implement the change. The complexity of introducing change is compounded when staff members who are to implement a change are also negativists toward the change. A superintendent from California, John Burns (personal communication, December 10, 1991), saw tragedy in resistance to change.

In my mind, it's a shame how many people are afraid of change, and it's a double shame when these people are teachers and/or educators. Educators are supposed to be the "eagles" not the "turkeys" of the world. They, above all others, should teach students to want and to dream and to strive. Yet I worked with too many teachers who feared changing their teaching assignments, or their classroom, or the site where they worked. What a tragedy. Again, I won't let myself fall into this trap and have made every attempt to prevent my management from losing their excitement for life and their job challenges.

Focusing upon the Future

To an elementary school principal from Michigan, the push for change, experimentation, and innovation is a way of life.

Staff has autonomy to seek new directions. I can't remember a time in thirteen years when I did not encourage experimentation. Although I push teachers to try new things (i.e., I observed whole-language teaching efforts as they were receiving training), I never zapped them for not being perfect. I encouraged them to reflect on their efforts and would follow up at a later time to verify their professional growth. I push myself to do risky things and share my anxieties with them when I do training for secondary staffs or parents. Another tough lesson I learned as a principal is that change takes time and that support must be there for the duration. As a teacher, I was always an early joiner to innovative efforts. The majority of my staff is not that way! Hence, I had to foster change quietly, consistently, persistently to gain the staff's ownership of particular ideas. Pats on the back for small steps have given people the courage to try more until their efforts became self-reinforcing because of the great results they saw in student learning. All administrivia is shared with teachers so there are no surprises. It's better to have too much information than not enough when dealing with change.

Perpetuating past practices is anathema to an elementary school principal from Wisconsin as the lessons from research have spurred him to seek new ways of improving classroom practices, instruction, and achievement.

Perhaps the most dangerous thing that we educators can do is to keep doing what we've always done. There has been a great deal of educational research done in the recent past. We need to be aware of this research and its implications as they affect instruction and learning. It seems right for a principal to nudge his staff to really want to investigate them, and then provide the opportunity to learn about them in depth so classroom practice changes. The outcome is improved instruction and enhanced achievement. We all realize that demographics are changing. It makes sense, then, that schools must change.

Supervising Change

Just turning teachers loose to do whatever they want to do is not good practice, as a superintendent from South Dakota pointed out. He expects to be kept informed of creative activities in his district and follows up with suggestions of his own.

I allow subordinates the freedom to explore new ideas and techniques. At the same time, I insist that they keep me fully informed about what they are doing, and I offer some suggestion. We have done many innovative things, and most of the ideas originated from other administrators or teachers. It is important to tap the creative juices of the whole staff.

Special efforts to gather new ideas at the end of a school year for implementation in the fall are made by Gail Gates (personal communication, March 9, 1991), a middle school principal from Louisiana. Her efforts are one means of transferring ideas from one year to the next and maintaining an impetus for improvement.

I involve the staff before making decisions. Often we meet to discuss school policies for possible revision, ways to improve teaching methods, how to increase parental involvement, how to increase the self-esteem of our student body, and other things that will improve the quality of education. At the end of each school year, I distribute an "End-of-the-Year Suggestion Sheet." On this form, each teacher is given an opportunity to write preferences regarding teaching and duty assignments, club sponsorship, and possible staff development topics. This form also has a section for comments concerning suggestions for improvement and recommendations for change. I carefully read and evaluate these and make some changes if feasible. All suggestions and recommendations are addressed at our first faculty meeting of the year so that the teachers know why or why not their input was acted upon. Not only do the activities include teachers in the decision-making process, but they also encourage the expression of new ideas and serve to further open the lines of communication between staff and administration.

RESISTANCE TO CHANGE

Advancements and improvement in other fields, as in medicine, may also face a welcoming public or negativists. The introduction of an oral vaccine for polio was accepted quite readily by a public whose doubt of the efficacy of the vaccine outweighed their fear of the disease; however, the release of minute quantities of fluoride into water systems created a furor in those who feared the consequences of such action and disregarded the assurances of dentists, researchers, and scientists. The lesson of the acceptance of the polio vaccine and rejection of fluoride is clear: Public acceptance of the idea of an innovation is the first, and perhaps the greatest, obstacle to change.

Why are members of a public resistant to change? In some persons, comfort is found in the known, the familiar, the status quo; in others, discomfort is found in the same, familiar surroundings and practices and trying new things leads to feelings of satisfaction. Listen to comments about a new idea and you are likely to hear comments such as "We tried that before," "By the time we figure out how to do that, some other tomfool idea will come along," "Who's got the time to do all that?" or "Why bother? Everything's fine just the way it is." What would the world be like had Edison been satisfied with candlelight? Had Salk and Sabin been satisfied that treatments for patients who had contracted the viral disease were sufficient for responding to polio? Had Mozart been satisfied with the music available for musicians to play? Had Monet and other Impressionists been satisfied with traditional painting styles? Had Ford, the Wright brothers, and other inventors been satisfied with traveling by horse and carriage? Had Bell and Marconi been satisfied with sending messages by mail? Had explorers been satisfied with letting the horizon limit their knowledge of the earth? Had Horace Mann been satisfied with the status of education in his day?

The Inevitability of Change

William J. Pappas (personal communication, January 21, 1992), a high school principal from Michigan, takes a long view and subsequently a proactive stance toward change.

> Because I believe change is inevitable and also a positive thing, I have been able to overcome the many obstacles and barriers that are quite common to the everyday operation of a high school administrator. I also believe that offering support, practicing equality for students and staff, and seeking excellence at all times have molded my administrative style. I have attempted always to look "down the road" five to ten years in order to make today's important decisions. What I do has an effect on students not only presently in school but for the many who will follow.

Typical Factors

Resistance to change is not limited to a single factor, mindset, or personality type. Administrators can gain some advantage in reducing resistance to change by looking for typical resistors, acknowledging their presence, and building positions that reduce resistance.

An example of overcoming resistance to change was provided by Gerald Freitag (personal communication, March 10, 1992), an administrator from Wisconsin.

> Another example was the weighted grades program that was met with a great deal of controversy. It evolved out of a discussion regarding the noticeable decrease in the number of individuals involved in some of our advanced programs. With the necessity to compete for scholarships, the need to maintain grade points had begun to have the effect of encouraging students not to extend themselves. The weighted grade system, although

not perfect, provided the incentive necessary for young people to take on the challenges. If successful, the rewards were far above what they could expect through any other avenue. If the success was only marginal, they still lost nothing but, instead, because they attempted something more difficult, really gained intellectually through the process. At first I was in the camp that opposed the change. I could see more negatives than positives to the weighted grade system. It seemed like a system steeped with bureaucracy that had inherent flaws and that showed no promise to accomplish what it was intended to accomplish. I must admit that a number of my colleagues convinced me to be open and to take a chance. Our board supported weighted grades, and so I, and a number others, worked with a number of our staff members to generate enough support to ensure that the implementation would be positive. I must admit, it did have the effect of buoying up and improving our advanced programs and in that regard helped a number of youngsters who might otherwise not have experienced the challenges provided by these programs. It would have been easy to continue the education we were providing. It was not inferior by any means; however, by making that next jump to another level, we provided advanced educational opportunities for individuals.

Values. A trip to garage sales should convince anyone that differences in values exist among people. One's educational philosophy or set of values may be opposed to a change. In such an instance, the key to reaching understanding rests upon a frank comparison of ideas, philosophical positions, and perceptions.

Knowledge. In some cases, those in opposition to a change may be merely uninformed. Information must be provided to individuals who lack knowledge of a change or innovation. Information about the benefits of fluoride treatment of drinking water did not dissuade many persons who disregarded one set of information and proposed their own facts in opposition to its use. How people are provided with information and who gives them the information may be as important as the kind and quality of information that is given them. Providing information to persons who have deep, inner fear of a proposed change is not likely to cause them to change their minds.

Norms. Individuals who like the current conditions may be opposed to new ideas that may change work procedures, expectations, and production levels. Persons interested in exploring new technology may threaten colleagues who fear that the implementation of new technology may force them to learn to adopt new technology into their daily work lives. The fears of failure in learning, of difficulty in learning, and of needing to spend more time in learning may create cyberphobia in individuals who are otherwise bright, productive, and supportive of new ideas but who may fear a decrease in their production levels in trying to master cyberspace. Because good technology programs can enable students to engage in cooperative learning projects, emphasize higher-level problem-solving skills as well as reinforce basic skills, create interactive learning environments built around real-world problems, support interactions among students and teachers, and are adaptable to a variety of learning styles (Jordan and Follman, 1993), educators should be encouraged to adapt technology to their teaching and administrative roles.

Past practice. "We've always done it this way." The cumulative weight of past practice is a heavy burden—too heavy for many to break. The insecurity brought about by a change must be attended to before habit can be broken and new skills introduced, taught, and, ultimately, learned, accepted, and expected. Inertia is a powerful force; its power is no less among persons faced with discarding old ways and adopting new ones.

Tradition. Honor and respect what is in the past but also look for ways to strengthen and improve upon past practices, procedures, and quality of performance. Appeal to a sense of pride in individuals who are bound by tradition is one means of gaining their support for a new idea. Refuting the accomplishments of past efforts will not likely win over traditionalists even though a considerable body of evidence could be used to argue for better ways of new practices over old ones.

An administrator from Utah revealed how he incorporated lessons that he had gained from good and bad experiences.

> I took into my assignment as a principal the attitude that I was not going to begin by making a clean sweep of everything that was done prior to my appointment but would take a year to analyze the situation at the school and begin to lay the groundwork for changes I felt would benefit the students and staff. During the course of my first year, I found it was valuable for me to share with members of the staff my philosophy regarding the operation of the school setting. I do not recall ever telling the staff that a problem must be approached in a certain way; rather, I went to the staff, stated the problem, and asked for their input. Together we made a decision. Throughout this process the staff, I feel, understood that the final decision would have to be mine. There were many successful experiences that came about due to teamwork with the staff.

Change itself. In some cases, a change or innovation is so complex, expensive, foreign, or unique that some individuals cannot embrace it. The broader in scope a change is, the more difficult its introduction, acceptance, and implementation. Proposed changes to modular scheduling, a four-period day, or a year-round school may be sufficient to illustrate how large-scale changes bring out opponents. If individuals sense that an innovation is set in its final form and that little or no input, other than acquiescence, is expected from them, the fallout is predictable for individuals will have no sense of ownership in the innovation.

Compounding factors. Many persons who resist change have more than one reason for resisting change. Thus, providing information to the uninformed may not be sufficient for they may have other, deeper, or hidden resistance. Nor do all persons resistant to a change share a single set of resistors. Some will resist because of tradition, and others for fear of having to change their ways of doing their jobs. In such cases, resistance to change in the two groups must be handled differently.

INTRODUCING CHANGE

Administrators may also follow general principles in introducing an innovation or change.

- Conduct a needs assessment to validate the necessity for improvement.
- Create conditions for staff members to introduce, develop, and accept ownership for change.
- Match the innovation with values already held.
- Catch the interest of individuals with a new idea.
- Keep comfort levels high.
- Minimize risks for adapters of an innovation or change.
- Reward adapters of an innovation or change.
- Enlist the support of key individuals—top administrators and influential members of the staff and community.
- Seek consensus about acceptance of an innovation.
- Avoid vote taking, as results from voting may split a staff into two or more factions.
- Show individuals how the change will not adversely affect their work load.
- Address the attitudes, fears, and reactions of individuals one to one.
- Monitor the acceptance level of individuals and groups throughout the process of change.
- Create and foster an open attitude toward changes in an innovation so that ideas may be added along the way.

Interpreting Resistance to Change

Most factors relative to the introduction, acceptance, and installation of an innovation or change are related to personal attitudes, beliefs, fears, likes and dislikes, and values as much as to the innovation itself. Teachers may "know" that being able to cruise the Internet is a valuable means of acquiring new ways of gathering and exchanging information, but teachers may be so overwhelmed by the prospect of learning new computer skills, software, terms, and techniques that the idea is rejected. Teachers may say, "I don't need that Internet stuff," when in reality they are saying, "I really should learn about the Internet because I know I'm falling behind what my colleagues know, but I'm afraid of learning about it."

In Virginia, a superintendent provided leadership for change by focusing energies upon change.

I work diligently to help my colleagues cope with change—changes in assumptions about reality linked with a realigning of the school district's purposes, cultures, and processes. Concomitantly, I try to provide leadership in shepherding our district through these times of significant transformation and renewal. In so doing, we focus our energies on moving our schools and district from current to future states, creating a vision of potential opportunities and instilling within colleagues the commitment to change, and instilling new cultures and strategies that focus energy and resources on school improvement.

TOTAL QUALITY MANAGEMENT

Is there an administrator in the 1990s who can think of quality and not think of W. Edwards Deming, the management wizard credited with transforming Japan into an industrial and economic superpower? Decades ago, "Made in Japan" was synonymous with poor quality. After the application of Deming's ideas, the products made by Honda, Sony, and other Japanese firms became renowned for their high quality.

Total Quality Management in Education

There are a few questions school administrators must continue to address: Can school administrators also produce high quality products? Why can't school personnel meet the needs of their customers—students—much better than they have? How can educators incorporate principles of TQM into schooling?

An elementary school principal from Indiana reported that she saw everyone as customers and focused upon their needs.

> I am able to get *all* customers—students, all staff, parents, and the community—involved in the exciting educational process. These groups are empowered to be their best, and we all work together to define and refine our program. Together we created a magnet school with science and technology emphases but also brought best practices (cooperative learning, discipline with dignity, process writing, whole language, thematic instruction, interdisciplinary teams, and so on. I find out what the many customers want—and then facilitate the processes to try to meet these wants.

For some administrators and educators, the concept of total quality management must loom like a specter—elusive, forbidding, and monstrous in nature and size. "Total" means that an entire organization must adapt itself to quality management; "quality" that everything done must be based on principles of quality; and "management," that accountability for results rests with administrators. A shift to TQM cannot be done lightly because it will raise many issues regarding expectations, commitment, and endurance.

Principles of Quality

In the early 1930s, Walter Shewart, an industrial statistician, proposed principles of quality control. He determined lower and upper limits for tasks and proposed that quality control could be enhanced by reacting to variations outside of such limits. Management focus was shifted from inspection at the end of the line to online variations so that quality was maintained throughout the process. Shewart's ideas about statistical analysis led to the advancement of quality as a science, of controlling processes, and of identifying acceptable quality levels for tasks. One of Shewart's disciples was W. Edwards Deming, who after World War II convinced Japanese industrial magnates that they should have a total commitment to quality and that all aspects of production should focus upon the consumer. After Japanese industrialists embraced the concept that the consumer was the most important part of production, the quality of Japanese goods soared. Still later, after Japanese products endeared themselves to consumers, U.S. industrialists hired themselves to Japan to learn their secrets—not realizing that the secrets lay in concepts propounded by Americans such as Shewart, Deming, and others interested in quality from start to finish. U.S. industrialists have since embraced the principle, as in Ford Motor Company's pledge that "Quality Is Job One."

The Origin of Quality

U.S. manufacturers had to learn that quality is established in the marketplace and not in executive suites. Consumers define quality by buying or not buying a product. The principle of "Doing a task right the first time" (Crosby, 1984) has to be established as "Doing a task well" to measure up to what consumers demand. "Doing it right the first time" means that a product will not be scrapped at the end of the line nor brought back for a refund if inspection fails to uncover a defect. Persons who have bought a new house can appreciate "Doing it right the first time" so that doors are hung properly, seals are thoroughly applied to fixtures and flashing, and sufficient coats of finish and paint are painted on surfaces.

Quality was defined by one corporate executive operationally: "Quality really is just doing what you said you were going to do . . . finding out what the customer wants, describing that, and then meeting that exactly" (Schaaf, 1991, 6). Educators too must be able to do what they say they are going to do and to find out what customers want, describe that, and then meet that exactly. Educators may claim greater difficulty in finding out what customers want, but that claim does not diminish their responsibility for seeking quality. Even auto makers do not have *a* customer but have customers who want choices from among inexpensive or luxury cars, family sedans or pickups, vans or station wagons, cars with or without sun roofs, and so on. Yet all customers who buy vehicles expect one feature: quality in the convertible, coupe, pickup, sedan, or van they purchase. All customers in schools expect the same feature of education: quality in instruction, learning, teaching, administration, and organization (Bradley, 1993; Neuroth, Plastrik, and Cleveland, 1992).

The Omnipresence of Quality

With the accent on quality in business and industry, the demand for quality has spilled over into public enterprises (Rosander, 1991). International competitiveness is so pervasive that the importance of quality will not disappear. Private producers of goods and services realize that having *satisfied* customers is not sufficient; customers must be *loyal*, so impressed and satisfied with the product or service that they return. Watch the ads on television that ask customers to switch telephone companies. Each company makes much the same pitch to consumers: Our company is the one that can meet your needs best, and if you sign on with us, we'll reduce your billing charges, especially for numbers you call frequently. In essence, long-distance firms promise *quality service* and *rewards for loyalty*, namely, use of the company's services at reduced charges.

The Role of Management

Deming argued that best efforts are embedded in a theory of management, not in piecemeal adjustments, slogans, and bit-by-bit tinkering. The pitch for long-distance telephone service illustrates the recognition of the need to satisfy customers and to court their loyalty. Can school administrators take a similar tack for their customers' satisfaction and loyalty by basing their quest for improvement and quality upon a theory of management? A basic theorem of TQM is that quality is the responsibility not of workers or lower-level managers but of top-level management. In schools, that theorem translates easily. If a district adopts a set of curriculum materials, teachers, aides, and other support personnel are not responsible for quality of the curriculum, since their job is to assist and to support the instructional process. Instead, top-level administrators of the district are responsible for quality because they have the responsibility to define quality in the curriculum and to improve delivery processes of that curriculum. Teachers, aides, and support personnel are responsible for their jobs—teaching and assisting in the instructional process—but accountability for results rests with administrators.

Some ideas frequently proposed for improvement and reform are, to the contrary, opposed by Deming. He decried the

> so-called merit system—actually, destroyer of people; management by objectives, management by the numbers, quotas, failure to optimize the various activities and divisions of a company as a system . . . worker training worker . . . [e]xecutives working with best efforts, trying to improve quality, the market, and profit, but working without guidance of profound knowledge. Tampering. (Deming, 1991, 9).

Administrators who are interested in increased productivity, higher quality of performance, and improvement in similar factors by establishing a system of merit pay might wish to rethink the wisdom of establishing such a system. Executives need "profound knowledge" to guide them in their decisionmaking rather than relying upon ideas that sound good, such as "worker training worker," or that are expedient, such as "tampering." Ill-trained mechanics who want to boost the gas mileage in their cars by tampering with a few parts might achieve better gas mileage or might cause malfunctions in fuel systems as easily. Administrators who want to tamper with the compensation system by setting aside money for a merit system may have to face lowered morale and dissatisfaction because of the anger, bickering, jealousy, and pettiness that would result from the distribution of a few dollars.

How can quality standards be set and met if top-level administrators cannot define quality (cannot establish standards for merit pay, for example) and simultaneously monitor performance so that meritorious accomplishments can be recognized? Demands for increased productivity, a merit pay system, and other "improvements" can be announced and installed readily in schools; however, their introduction does not necessarily lead to desired improvements. The latter must be designed by top-level administrators who must be able to unleash forces that elevate people and to reduce forces that, as Deming said, destroy people. To accomplish quality, administrators need profound knowledge, not just concepts that are bandied about as reforms or "just seem to be right to me."

A superintendent from New Hampshire, Gerald Daley (personal communication, February 24, 1992), indicated how expectations for improvement from top-level management can be realized.

Educational leaders provide direction for their schools. They set goals and hold people accountable for reaching them. They have high expectations for both personnel and students. They care about people and they care about results. The prime expectation that I have for everyone in our district, from student to superintendent, is that he or she will constantly strive to improve . . . . Our people understand that no matter how good they are, there is always room for growth, always room for improvement. Just knowing that improvement is expected is often enough to bring it about. Four years ago the dropout rate at our high school began to increase. Without any urging from me the high school principal declared the increased rate unacceptable and set about to improve it. Since then the rate has dropped steadily to its lowest point in over ten years. Recently our special education staff embarked on a lengthy process of self-improvement when it decided it could deliver its services more effectively. Their self-initiated project involves teachers, parents, board members, and administrators, all dedicated to improving the way special education operates in the district. They know improvement is expected here, and they are working to make it happen.

Profound Knowledge

Four elements comprise profound knowledge: (1) appreciation for a system, (2) theory of variation, (3) theory of knowledge, and (4) knowledge of psychology. The elements of profound knowledge are inseparable and incomplete without each other. For example, administrators who understand variations among people, their assignments, need dispositions, and numerous other factors and who understand psychology will not expend their efforts upon improving rating scales of staff members' performance but, instead, will expend their efforts upon exploring factors that attend to each individual's job, motivation, and needs and fit with the system. An underlying assumption of rating staff performance is that criteria of performance can be set, observed, collected, monitored, and graded. A few minutes of conversation with teachers will produce evidence that criteria of performance are seldom set or adhered to and that little, or no, time is given to observing, collecting data, monitoring, giving feedback, and otherwise improving performance (Juran, 1989).

At the time of annual performance review, an administrator of a unit came to staff members individually and announced that he wanted staff members, exclusive of self, to rank order other members of the unit. When questioned about the validity and reliability of rank ordering without prior notification, the administrator replied, "I've thought about it a lot." Discussion with self was the administrator's justification. Few people lose arguments to themselves. On what basis could individuals be asked to rank order the performance of their peers at the end of the year without prior knowledge of the task from day one? This administrator placed total emphasis upon the rank ordering of staff members and gave little or no recognition to the need for information for any kind of personnel appraisal. The administrator lacked profound knowledge about the effect of such rank ordering upon members of the unit and other adverse affects that might be expected from knowledge of psychology and other elements.

Administrators need to function on the basis that whatever actions they take will cause improvement, and that if improvement is not forthcoming, another change will be made. "I think, therefore it is," to paraphrase Descartes, is poor logic for administrators to follow.

Appreciation for a system. Administrators need to understand how all parts and subparts fit into a system (Senge, 1990). Much as traffic engineers must understand how all the streets, boulevards, expressways, interchanges, one-way streets, dangerous intersections, speed limits, amount of traffic, vehicular patterns, public transportation, intended housing developments, and condition of roadways fit together, administrators must understand how a change in one part of the system interacts with other parts. The introduction of the middle school concept will, to a greater or lesser extent, affect everyone in a district. The decision to adopt the middle school concept will affect grade-level organization, teaching assignments, attitudes about instruction, interscholastic athletic competition, approaches to curriculum, and how students' needs are viewed, to name a few areas. Introducing only the teacher-advisee concept into a traditional junior high school is an example of "tampering" and is not likely to shift much of anything toward the ideals of middle-level education. Individuals who are resistant to change may conclude that there is really not much that is different about middle-level education if having a daily ten-minute period for teacher-advisee is all that is required for a shift to middle-level education. Advocates of middle-level education could become incensed over such a feeble effort. Administrators who desire improvement and change must know and appreciate the interrelationships of curriculum, instruction, developmental stages of students, and staff members' need for inservice training.

The greater the complexity of a system, the greater is the need for appreciation of the system. A nation's Olympic team is composed of many persons, some who work closely together, as a relay team or pair of ice skaters, while others compete as individuals in events. The team may be successful but not necessarily because all athletes train at the same time in the same way. Organizations as school districts, however, are systems that need a high degree of coordination and the support of all working together for the common good (Schlechty, 1993; Weisbord, 1987). Within school systems, administrators' efforts to rank people, attendance centers, or units fail to capitalize upon human resources but, instead, merely make comparisons that reveal nothing about past performance or predict performance in the future. Conflict is generally introduced when nonuseful comparisons are made as individuals or members of units seek to get a higher ranking, develop bitterness about perceived poor ranking or envy toward those with higher rankings, replace concern over quality with getting a higher ranking, and wind up with lower morale and job satisfaction.

Knowledge of variation. Administrators must recognize that variations exist—that no two people can perform at the same level or that a program can be equally successful under different conditions. What needs to be determined is whether a system is performing as can be predicted from past performance; if not, actions must be taken to determine how much variation exists and what actions, if any, need to be taken to bring the system back into stable condition. Two types of error can result in trying to make an improvement: (1) treating any perceived problem as emanating from a special cause when the problem is the result of common causes and (2) treating any perceived problem as emanating from common causes when the problem is the result of a special cause. Administrators must learn to discern between common and special causes.

Discernment is a function of gathering and using data, getting information from diverse sources, engaging others in a cooperative analysis of a perceived problem, and using information to conduct an analysis of the problem (Naisbitt and Auburdene, 1985). Some foresight is required, of course, as a system of collecting information must be in place. Information collected over time will be of much greater value than information collected from only a short duration, and so administrators must have an ongoing data collection system. The nature of information available is an important factor to consider; for instance, a compilation of information may support the introduction of a new language arts program. Assurances from a publisher, critiques from experts, and testimonials from users may be the best available information but may still not result in a prediction that the language arts program may be a pronounced improvement over the program in place. In short, the principle of knowledge of variation behooves administrators to examine all sides of a question lest, for example, a small drop in test scores is misinterpreted as a fatal plunge.

Theory of knowledge. Another of the principles of TQM is the *theory of knowledge*. Administrators are typically confronted with deciding between at least two choices: standing pat or opting for a new program, approach, or method. A decision to stand pat or to choose Program Alpha, Program Beta, or Program Omega is based upon a determination that improvement will result. Thus administrators are frequently engaged in the prediction of outcomes—that a new approach to the teaching of mathematics will increase student learning, teacher job satisfaction, and patron support. One approach often recommended to educators is to make a pilot study of a program under consideration before introducing it full scale. The theory of knowledge informs administrators to make careful study of the results of a pilot program. If inadequate controls, poor sampling techniques, or other slipshod methods of evaluation are employed, the results of a pilot study may do little more than to pay lip service to the experiment. How often have promising programs been introduced only to fall short of their promise? Or, even worse perhaps, how often have promising programs been introduced without any efforts to determine their value? Similarly, programs that are implemented successfully require careful planning, extensive data gathering, input from many persons and groups, exhausting attention to detail, and a commitment over time. One superintendent reported how a technology plan extended over six years and success was determined not from day one but over those six years (VanSciver, 1994). Innovations or changes that are proposed upon nonexistent or poor databases, theory, or knowledge have diminished chance for success.

Successful administrators have a never-ending thirst for knowledge, an insatiable quest for better ways of conducting operations, and a continuing desire for personal growth. They look for ways of self-renewal, to network with peers, to stretch their level of understanding, to explore new fields of knowledge, and to invite others to join them on their voyages into new territories. Successful administrators will seek input from a variety of sources on important matters before making decisions and will base their decisions upon informed knowledge, sound theory, and best practice (Kaufman and Zahn, 1993).

Using available knowledge to improve performance on the job was reported by David Haney (personal communication, March 9, 1992), a superintendent from North Dakota. "I make a conscious effort to improve. For example, one of my responsibilities is to evaluate the principals. I did not feel that I was providing them appropriate guidance. I found the solution to my problem by completing the National Association of Secondary School Principals assessment training program."

Knowledge of psychology. Administrators work with, through, and for people. Administrators work daily with superordinates, peers, subordinates, and individuals external to their system. Administrators must also work through people, since all people in a system must work together to accomplish the goals of their organizations; no administrator, working alone, can accomplish what the collective whole can

(Feigenbaum, 1983). Administrators also work *for* people, not only for their superordinates and employers but for their subordinates as well. The concept of servant leadership is fundamental to developing successful interpersonal relationships (Sergiovanni, 1991). An elementary principal from Iowa described her responsibility for and attitudes about leading her staff toward change.

> Being a lover of change—believing that the most efficient and effective route to change is through participation of everyone every day. The leader that is a lover of change is enthusiastic about change and its effect on the future of the school. Efficacious leaders innovate and improve education for all students. Leaders of change influence the metabolism of the building and stir emotions. They look for incremental change—small steps that eventually move the organization to the goal. Lovers of change have a tolerance for well intended failure. Change occurs slowly, may fail, but most importantly it must take place in an atmosphere where failure is accepted. More people rather than fewer develop the energy to create change. Leaders are successful when they seek help and assistance from everyone, letting them produce their best and then acknowledging their accomplishments. By doing this the leader creates an action plan for students, staff, and community that personifies teamwork, a dignity for the teaching-learning process, and a spirit of trust, cooperation, and commitment.

Many theorists have recognized the importance of good interpersonal relationships, and the concept is certainly not new. Halpin (1966), in his study of leadership, emphasized two dimensions: (1) initiating structure, a leader's behavior in delineating the relationship between self and workers and establishing channels of communication, methods of procedure, and patterns of communication; and (2) consideration, establishing friendship, mutual trust, rapport, and respect between self and members of the group. Halpin's work led to further studies of leadership and its impact on leadership in organizations. The theories proposed by Douglas McGregor—Theory X and Theory Y—were based upon how administrators view the attitudes, integrity, and value of others (McGregor, 1960). Getzels and Guba identified two important dimensions of an organization: the needs of the organization itself and the need dispositions of individuals within the organization. Abraham Maslow articulated a hierarchy of needs that places a compelling value upon basic physiological and psychological needs. To date, no theorist has ever advanced the proposition that all people are the same and should be treated as such, or that people are exactly as an administrator believes them to be and will respond exactly as the administrator expects and demands.

Knowledge of learners' developmental processes and needs are also important. Visit the classrooms of teachers who are and are not able to motivate students for a reminder of the value of knowledge of child or adolescent psychology. Exemplary teachers recognize students' different learning styles, needs, feelings, and moods. To one student, a verbal stroke by a teacher is appropriate; to another, a flickering glance of approval from a teacher is sufficient to bring satisfaction. Research from the effective schools movement has documented the need for schools to be safe places (i.e., a form of documentation of Maslow's hierarchy of needs), and good teachers will have order and other features that produce a healthy learning climate (Herman, 1993; Murgatroyd and Morgan, 1992).

Administrators must bring their knowledge of staff members' and students' developmental tasks, needs, wants, dispositions, attitudes, learning styles, and other elements into a unified whole to bring about improvement in the organization (Schlechty, 1990). What is improvement? What if the introduction of a new mathematics program produces higher scores on standardized tests yet alienates students in math classes so that registration in elective and advanced classes drops off and students vow never to take another math class? By the same token, math teachers might be disillusioned over a math program that diminishes their creativity, sets unrealistic expectations for their students to achieve, or diametrically opposes principles the teaching staff has adopted. Improvement in math scores is to be sought; nevertheless, other outcomes must be weighed.

Working collaboratively with others has led to success for a high school principal from Oklahoma. "Providing the staff with information and findings from research that will affect the school positively is fairly easy, but without commitment on their part to make things happen, nothing is accomplished. Thus, it is through a collaborative effort that I have experienced success."

Knowledge of motivation is a prerequisite to improvement. Herzberg's motivation and hygiene theory, for example, emphasizes that extrinsic motivators are not as longlasting as intrinsic ones. Some factors are likely to be potential dissatisfiers, such as school policy. A set of policies adopted by a school board may bring some satisfaction to employees who may acknowledge the board's obligation to have written policies in place, but the chance of a set of policies bringing dissatisfaction is greater because as individuals feel thwarted by a policy, believe a policy to be unjustly or indiscriminately administered, or have their personal needs blocked by a decision based upon policy, then dissatisfaction occurs. Much of the mystery of motivation must be mastered and removed if administrators are to achieve demonstrable, lasting, and significant improvement.

Social psychologists have documented the importance of working for the common good, engaging individuals in cooperative efforts that let them release their innate talents, recognizing individuals' worth so that their self-esteem is enhanced, and making work and learning a joy rather than a hodge-podge of onerous tasks. Much of success in society seemingly rests upon competition and external rewards for best, biggest, or most, yet awards given to the few diminish the importance of others. Over time, consistent focus upon extrinsic rewards erodes intrinsic motivation, job satisfaction, self-esteem, and confidence in administrators' understanding of what they are supposed to be doing.

The father of scientific management, Frederick Winslow Taylor, gained fame for the principles of production that he established for industry. Not surprisingly, the next administrative school of thought was introduced by Mary Parker Follett, who stressed the human element in organizations. Other theorists followed with what is commonly referred to as the behavioral sciences approach, and theorists and practitioners alike are struggling to isolate ideal administrative and organizational approaches. One field of knowledge that should not be overlooked is that of psychology, since lasting improvements can come only from within the minds and wills of individuals.

Deming's Fourteen Points

Deming (1986) himself advanced a theory of management in fourteen points:

1. Make improvement of product and service a constant goal. An organization's purpose is to stay operational. For example, the role of a business is to stay in business and provide jobs rather than to make money.
2. Adopt a new management philosophy that is based on quality. The world is in a new, international economy. Managers must not tolerate poor workmanship and service.
3. Halt the practice of inspection to achieve quality. The need for mass inspection at the end of a process should be eliminated by improvement of the process of the organization.
4. Stop awarding business only on the basis of low bid or price tag. Instead, seek suppliers with the best quality and maintain a long-term relationship of loyalty and trust with them.
5. Improve production and service continuously so that quality and productivity are improved. Thus costs and waste will also be decreased.
6. Start on-the-job training so that workers are properly trained.
7. Provide leadership by helping people do a better job with available resources. Both managers and subordinates need proper supervision.
8. Increase effectiveness by driving out fear. Quality and productivity will improve if employees feel secure about what they are to do, are not afraid to ask questions, and are encouraged to try new and better methods of performing their jobs.
9. Break down intra-organizational barriers. Employees in all units must work as a team to improve quality of product and service.
10. Eliminate slogans, exhortations, and targets for employees. Because most causes of poor quality and productivity are system-related rather than employee related, slogans, and so on are ill-directed.
11. Eliminate numerical standards and quotas, management by objectives, management by numbers, and numerical goals. To reach numerical goals, individuals may sacrifice important ends.
12. Abolish annual or merit ratings, management by objectives, and management by numbers that devalue employee's pride and sense of accomplishment in their work.

13. Initiate programs directed toward training, retraining, self-improvement, statistical techniques, and teamwork.
14. Make everyone in the organization responsible for transforming the organization, the unit, and personal role to improve quality of product and service.

Ideal Practices

What should leaders be doing? Deming (1986) proposed qualities that leaders must have to focus upon ideal management practices:

- Understand how the work of their group fits into the aims of the company.
- Work with preceding stages and with following stages.
- Try to create joy in work for everybody. Try to optimize the education, skills, and abilities of everyone and help everyone to improve.
- Serve as coaches and counselors, not as judges.
- Use figures to help understand their people and themselves. Understand variation. Use statistical calculation to learn who, if anybody, is outside the system in need of special help.
- Work to improve the system that they and their people work in.
- Create trust.
- Do not expect perfection.
- Listen and learn.

To sum up ideas of Total Quality Management, administrators must stop focusing upon the judgment of results but instead must start focusing upon the improvement of process. That is the chief purpose of administrators—to focus upon improving the processes of learning, teaching, and doing whatever tasks must be done (Fullan, 1993).

The foundation for achieving that purpose is good, effective relationships between administrator and subordinates. Teacher empowerment, quality circles, site-based management, and other approaches will have short-term impact unless sound relationships exist between administrators and their subordinates (Herman, 1993). From one study, ten managerial habits and practices were identified that mark foundational relationships (A Checklist of Qualities, 1984):

1. Provides clear direction and purpose.
2. Encourages open communication—vertical and horizontal.
3. Coaches and supports supervisees.
4. Provides objective recognition of achievement.
5. Establishes and maintains monitoring and control of operations.
6. Selects the right individuals for positions.
7. Understands financial implications of decisions.

8. Creates a climate for innovation and change.
9. Gives clear directions for actions to be taken when needed.
10. Maintains a high level of integrity.

The search for quality extends over time; the goal cannot be reached without long-term commitments to improving communication patterns, shifting power and authority (Naisbitt and Auburdene, 1985), maintaining constancy of purpose (Levering, 1988), and focusing upon organizational patterns, relationships (Schmoker and Wilson, 1993), and processes (Byham, 1989; Covey, 1989; Kilmann, 1988). Administrators may need to examine the nature of their relationships with subordinates and seek to build relationships that create trust among them (Schmoker and Wilson, 1993), energize them to seek solutions to problems cooperatively, and enhance their self-respect (Jablonski, 1991; Levering, 1988). Habits of administrators (i.e., typical ways of thinking about and treating subordinates) must be consistent with ways of establishing and maintaining effective, efficient, and productive working environments. Administrators who are seeking to improve conditions can examine five tracks: (1) the organization's culture, (2) the administrator's skills for solving problems, (3) the group's approaches to making decisions and taking action, (4) strategic choices and structural arrangements for reaching those choices, and (5) the purpose and nature of the reward system (Kilmann, 1988). Administrators who are successful in bringing about changes and improvements, in installing innovative projects, in changing their organization's culture (Kaufman and Zahn, 1993), and in continuing the search for quality have learned to apply human motivators that tap employees' needs for fairness, honesty, quality, self-esteem, and potential. In the end, quality consists of doing the right thing (what) in the right way (how) consistently over time.

SUMMARY

Successful administrators are in line with key administrative and organizational targets of the 1990s—innovation, quality, and improvement. They seek continuous improvement of programs in their schools so that educational opportunities can be further extended to all learners. Successful administrators resist holding fast to the status quo that is, at best, the mark from which to begin to launch new endeavors. Instead, administrators foster change, enlist support from others to effect substantive change, and focus upon the future by encouraging experimentation, developmental growth of staff members, and innovative efforts. Over the years, successful administrators have developed strategies for building a quest for improvement into the climate of their schools because they acknowledge the inevitability of change.

The writings of W. Edwards Deming and his followers contain many points that school administrators embrace. For example, they believe the "most efficient and effective route to change is through participation of everyone every day," as expressed by an elementary school principal from Iowa. She did not refer to quality circles or other terms associated with total quality management, but like other successful administrators, she was well aware of factors associated with change and the process of change. But most importantly, successful school administrators recognize the need for innovation, change, and continuous improvement through collaborative efforts to enhance teaching and learning.

REFERENCES

Bonstingl, J. J. (1992). *Schools of quality: An introduction to total quality management in education.* Alexandria, VA: Association for Supervision and Curriculum Development.

Bradley, L. H. (1993). *Total quality management for schools.* Lancaster, PA: Technomic Publishing Co.

Byham, W. C. (1989). *Zapp! The lightning of empowerment.* Pittsburgh, PA: Development Dimensions International Press.

A checklist of qualities that make a good boss. (1984, November). *Nation's Business, 72,* 100.

Costello, R. W. (1993, November). Using business criteria to make technology decisions in a school district. *T.H.E. Journal, 21*(4), 105-108.

Covey, S. R. (1989). *The 7 habits of highly effective people.* New York: Simon & Schuster.

Crosby, P. B. (1984). *Quality without tears: The art of hassle-free management.* New York: McGraw-Hill.

Deming, W. E. (1991). Foundation for management of quality in the Western world. In *An introduction to total quality for schools.* Arlington, VA: American Association of School Administrators.

Deming, W. E. (1986) *Out of the crisis.* Boston: Massachusetts Institute of Technology, Center for Advanced Engineering Study.

Feigenbaum, A. V. (1983). *Total quality control.* New York: McGraw-Hill.

Fullan, M. G., & Miles, M. B. (1992). Getting reform right: What works and what doesn't. *Phi Delta Kappan, 73*(10), 744-752.

Halpin, A., W. (1966). *Theory and research in administration.* New York: Macmillan.

Herman, J. J. (1993). *Holistic quality: Managing, restructuring, and empowering schools.* Newbury Park, CA: Corwin Press

Jablonski, J. R. (1991). *Implementing total quality management: An overview.* San Diego: Pfeiffer.

Jordan, W. R., & Follman, J. M. (1993). *Using technology to improve teaching and learning.* Greensboro, NC: Southeastern Regional Vision for Education. (ERIC Document Reproduction Service No. ED 353 930).

Juran, J. M. (1989). *Juran on leadership for quality: An executive handbook.* New York: Macmillan.

Kaufman, R., & Zahn, D. (1993). *Quality management plus: The continuous improvement of education.* Newbury Park, CA: Corwin Press.

Kilmann, R. H. (1988). *Beyond the quick fix*. San Francisco: Jossey-Bass.

Levering, R. (1988). *A great place to work: What makes some employers so good (and most so bad)*. New York: Random House.

McGregor, D. (1960). *The human side of enterprise*. New York: McGraw-Hill.

Murgatroyd, S., & Morgan, C. (1992). *Total quality management and the school*. Philadelphia: Open University Press.

Naisbitt, J., & Auburdene, P. (1985). *Re-inventing the corporation: Transforming your job and your company for the new information society*. New York: Warner Books.

Neuroth, J., Plastrik, P., & Cleveland, J. (1992). *Total quality management TQM handbook: Applying the Baldrige criteria to schools*. Arlington, VA: American Association of School Administrators.

Rosander, A. C. (1991). *Deming's 14 points applied to services*. New York: Marcel Dekker.

Schaaf, D. (1991): Beating the drum for quality. *Training, 28*(3), 5-8.

Schlechty, P. C. (1990). *Schools for the 21st century: Leadership implications for educational reform*. San Francisco: Jossey-Bass.

Schlechty, P. C. (1993, November). Shared decisions that count. *The School Administrator, 50*(10),20 -23.

Schmoker, M. J., & Wilson, R. B. (1993). *Total quality education: Profiles of schools that demonstrate the power of Deming's management principles*. Bloomington, IN: Phi Delta Kappa.

Senge, P. M. (1990). *The fifth discipline: The art and practice of the learning organization*. New York: Doubleday.

Senge, P. M. (1993, Spring). Transforming the practice of management. *Human Resource Development Quarterly, 4,* 5-32.

Sergiovanni, T. J. (1991). *The principalship: A reflective practice perspective* (2nd ed.). Boston, MA: Allyn and Bacon.

VanSciver, J. H. (1994). Using a strategic plan to promote technology in less wealthy rural school districts. *T. H. E. Journal, 22*(2), 72-73.

Weisbord, M. R. (1987). *Productive workplaces: Organizing and managing for dignity, meaning and community*. San Francisco: Jossey-Bass.

8

RISK TAKING

Have you ever bragged about being able to perform some service or activity but immediately began to back-pedal when you found the person you were addressing took you up on the offer? This is part of what we found when administrators defined themselves as "risk takers." Not that they wanted to be categorized as something else; they wanted the opportunity to qualify their definition.

We were encouraged with the number of administrators who said they were risk takers. Generally those indicating some level of risk taking as an attribute of their effectiveness seemed to be bragging. It was as though they were trying to convince a group of job interviewers that they were the right person for the position, since the district obviously did not have a resident risk taker and was in dire need of one.

A consultant with Harold Webb Associates and prior superintendent in Virginia wrote that he is willing to take risks for education. He finds most of his colleagues are very conservative and traditional in their thinking. That is why he thrives on impossible situations. He is a strong believer that leaders can make a difference. His philosophy is that "everyone has twenty-four hours; some people sleep longer than others."

There are dangers in being a risk taker. You might be taking the risk by yourself. Not everyone feels comfortable being around a risk taker especially if some controversial issues threatens to heat up the environment. We found the majority of administrators who said they were risk takers clarified their position. They said they took "calculated risks." Doug Cobb (personal communication, December 31, 1991), for example, a superintendent in Wyoming said: "I am a risk taker, but I will tell you that before I take any risks, they are carefully planned. I look at the timing, people involved, and the situation so that when I do take a risk, I know where I am going and I have carefully studied and am prepared to make any adjustments that may need to be made."

Are risk takers the same as calculated risk takers? Calculated risk takers tend to be more analytical in their approach. They do not want to be wrong, so they look for all relevant data, tend to be slower coming to a conclusion, and do not brag about the particular risk they are taking. Is that a risk? Must a real risk come from inadequate information and a genuine uncertainty about the results?

Why would calculated risk taking be a characteristic of outstanding school administrators? Because any risk taking as an administrator can cause political or career catastrophes. Imagine convincing your board or staff to support a course of action that might encourage the "nay-sayers" to take an active role in trying to negate the administrator's intentions. Wouldn't it be easier and less threatening to take small steps and not threaten the equilibrium?

A midwestern superintendent made an interesting observation. He not only discussed how risks might lead to failure but also talked about risks leading to success. First, he listed a belief statement about taking risks and moving ahead. It was a matter of envisioning and acting on ideas—probably not a risk at all. It was his belief that most, if not all, people have the capacity to dream big dreams and formulate wonderful ideas about desired or desirable future conditions. The differences between and among people allow some to speak with others about their dreams and to act on them, whereas many others never utter a word. He said that perhaps the fear of failure or the fear of success keeps people from moving ahead. He really did not know.

Yet, he said, risk taking is a characteristic of all leaders. They study the issues and calculate a plan of action. Action involves taking risks, and he has always taken the risks necessary to move a program or an organization forward.

Some individuals may insulate themselves and their actions from becoming too successful because success would require them to behave differently, they say. Imagine administrators building their lives around a comfortable level of success and suddenly finding themselves facing a fantastic, successful future. Picture how they would act. Would they live in the same neighborhood, drive the same car, cultivate the same friends? Some successes might force them to live outside their comfort zones. Just thinking about such change creates tension that causes some individuals to retreat from too much success. It is easier to accommodate modest success and not face the wrenching issues that come with superior performance.

Validation of structured interviews found that people who are successful talk differently than those who are not as successful. Successful people typically talk about wanting to be in a position to help support and direct others to become successful. From intervening with students, to providing a supporting environment, to providing an atmosphere where staff members can become role models and encouragers of student growth, successful administrators develop a vocabulary and vision that others can understand as well as appreciate.

All people have comfort zones from which they operate. They may make a few side trips and excursions out of their comfort zones, but these forays are usually short lived. Risk takers, on the other hand, are spending more time out of the comfort zone and may, in fact, be jeopardizing the comfort zone of students, parents, and citizens in their school or district. When others are stressed about an action or position being espoused by a risk taker, a significant number of these individuals may cause difficulty for the administrator.

Christine Johnson (personal communication, October 30, 1991), a high school principal in Colorado, states: "I view myself as a principle-centered leader. I have committed myself to doing what I feel is right as opposed to what is easy or traditional. Often this involves some risk taking and controversy; but I feel overall that a true test of my decisions and actions is how aligned these are with my principles."

A number of administrators said they were successful because they fostered and supported a climate that encouraged risk taking. Through an active encounter with risk taking, activities and policies were supported and encouraged, moving the agenda forward.

An assistant superintendent in Washington, Mark Mitrovich (personal communication, April 27, 1992), said:

> Many years ago, I read a magazine article that discussed a study undertaken to determine the person most qualified by training and experience to be president of the United States. The choice was Henry Cummins, the president of Cummins Diesel Engines. When asked what made him so successful, Mr. Cummins responded that he had the ability to choose the right people for the right job and then recognize them for their accomplishments. This, in turn, had made his company very successful.

> Over time, I have come to appreciate the wisdom of his words. I believe that by creating a climate that encourages risk taking, supports success, and recognizes setbacks as true learning experiences, the fear of change is reduced significantly. Rather than back away from challenges, we meet them with an attitude that sees them as open doors for growth. My part in this process is fostering that climate while providing the instructional leadership that gives a sense of vision to our total endeavors.

Some administrators felt that empowering teachers to make decisions helped to foster an atmosphere of risk taking. A few administrators said that even though empowerment was a concept on which the jury was still out, they felt sufficient risks were built into the system to bring it to a screeching halt.

A middle school principal in Nebraska talked about the climate he was able to establish in the buildings he has managed. He thought he was nominated because of the climate he had been able to create in the buildings in which he had been a part. The climate was established by empowering teachers to make decisions that affected them and by requiring teachers to be risk takers, to be creative thinkers, to work in collegial relationships, to be a part of a collaborative team, and to take responsibility for the decisions they made. Creating this type of climate for faculty members also helped create a positive and caring environment for the students with whom they worked.

He also believed his approach to problems contributed to his nomination. He approaches all problems as a challenge to learn, grow, and change for the better. Problems are not something to fear. He also believes in being a "good finder" and encourages people to focus on their positive talents in becoming the best they can be. Finally, he believes in the power of modeling. Principals must be models for the faculty in their relationships with people.

Robert Reeves (personal communication, February 13, 1992), a superintendent in California, talked about creating an environment that encouraged innovation where risk taking is rewarded. He echoes the culture of a number of innovative corporations that have built a strong research and development component focusing on rewarding employees to take risks.

Imagine working in an organization that wanted to become a leader in its field but punished its employees for taking risks. That is not how this superintendent operates.

> In the quest for excellence, we are always looking for a better way. Our district is very dynamic. I have created an environment where innovation and risk taking are rewarded. We believe in delegated management where department managers are responsible for their departments and principals are responsible for their schools. They are accountable for their budgets and all decision making at their site. Beyond the general operating budget and allocations for professional development, resources are targeted to support new, creative, innovative ideas—entrepreneurism is valued, appreciated, and rewarded.
>
> Moving to a "win-win" model of bargaining and entering into a new realm of trust was hard for the system and me—but it worked! Our teachers were ready for a more positive environment because of years of being treated as professionals through staff development and site decision making.

When administrators say they encourage risk taking among their staff, they are not looking for someone to put their programs or personnel in jeopardy; they are looking for their staff to open up to innovation. What could create a more stagnant environment than a staff that says, "But we have always done it this way?" How refreshing to mold a staff that says, "Let's give it a try; what do we have to lose? We might lose more by not trying."

To get to that position, an administrator must have developed a reputation for rewarding performance that looks at ways to improve situations rather than to accommodate them. The administrator must have established a history of not punishing people for taking calculated risks. If he or she is not consistent in wanting personnel to risk for improvements, risking will not be high on anyone's agenda.

If you look at what a school or district is accomplishing, you will be looking at what the district rewards. If administrators reward initiative, innovation, and risk taking, that is what they will get. If those attributes are channeled into practices that support and encourage exceptional student achievement, that is what they will get.

A junior high school principal in Massachusetts believes the principal holds the key. Principals are responsible for the climate of their schools, he believes. If they value diversity and encourage risk taking, a possibility exists that some of that may rub off. Without the principal's lead, none will occur. Common wisdom has it that teachers seem not to be risk takers, but in the twenty years that he and his teachers have worked together, they have tolerated his Friday activity days, fine and performing arts assemblies, week-long survival program in the woods, an insistence upon a strong social awareness, a community "call-in" program, and final evaluation letters from graduating eighth graders.

What is most outstanding about his staff is that for the twenty years they have had an interdisciplinary team concept; they held on to daily team planning times and have used them as intended, for team planning and student and parent conferences. Teachers were "empowered" long before they knew it was a gift disguised as a problem.

Just the act of living is a risk. Imagine the faltering flight of the nestling that lays its life on the line to try its wings. Where in the professional work of administrators is such a potential sacrifice required? Although some administrators are reticent about taking major risks, they do feel risks are something in which everyone should share.

Glenn E. Jonagan (personal communication, November 4, 1991), a middle school principal in Missouri, wrote:

> My leadership style is built on the concept of participatory management that assures that each teacher, student, and school patron shares in the responsibility of decisionmaking. My main function as a principal is to act as a facilitator and create a climate where failure is not fatal, with the reminder that to live is to risk . . . to risk is to take action . . . to take action is to lead.

Fear freezes action! In fact, for many, fear and inaction coexist; yet fear and action cannot exist together for long. Often the fear of failure or fear itself saps a leader's initiative to the degree that he or she is immobilized. Risk taking, on the other hand, can actually thwart fear and help leaders move ahead—however tentatively. This forward movement to some extent negates the fear holding them from action. When action begins, the fear recedes.

Stuart Berger (personal communication, January 2, 1992), a superintendent in Kansas, wrote:

> What success I have had stems from being a risk taker. Often, I have tried something new; occasionally, it did not work. Often, I ignored the caution of others; occasionally, I have paid the price. But ultimately, no matter how great the commitment and how sound the vision, progress occurs only through strong individuals taking risks.

People who take calculated risks are growth oriented. They are actually designing a course of action that will force them to meet new challenges, and for some of which they may have minimal preparation. It is the anticipation of challenges that focuses the attention and mental energy of the risk taker and provides the element of excitement that makes the risk worthwhile. Add to that excitement the potential for moving forward an agenda that will benefit people, and you have a mix of risk and altruism that is the catalyst for action.

A superintendent in Maryland said that if he has been successful, it is because he has been blessed with working with enthusiastic, energetic, creative, and capable people who are dedicated and successful. His job is to create and maintain an environment where people are free to take some risks and grow. David Kelley, a professor at Stanford University and CEO of IDEO, a design firm in Palo Alto, California, is quoted in the July 4, 1994, issue of *Industry Week*.

> People who have been successful are not mindful of how they got that way. To learn, fail. When a design fails, you learn its maximum performance. If nothing ever breaks you don't really know how strong it is. Strike out fear of failure and build a culture that allows it. Reward success and failure equally—punish inactivity. To engineer is human.

With a slightly different spin, Leslie Anderson (personal communication, October 14, 1991), a middle school principal in North Dakota says: "We try to operate on the edge of our competence which causes some setbacks, frustrations and mistakes. We do not perceive these as failures but, rather, as learning experiences to help us to provide a better program."

To be known as a risk taker is to be known as an individual who makes a certain amount of false starts and mistakes. Being known as a risk taker can provide a certain amount of insulation, however. There is an expectation in the eyes of the beholder that risk takers will make a certain number of mistakes. Risk taking becomes the rule, not the exception. If mistakes are expected and anticipated, why not take the risk? What do you have to lose?

A high school principal in Minnesota takes risks and encourages other to do the same. He makes mistakes—large and small—admits openly to them (privately or publicly depending on where and how the mistakes were made), takes personal responsibility for them without making excuses or giving explanations, and strives to do better. He expects and encourages others to do likewise. He believes that of all the institutions, a school should be a model of self-inquiry, a model think tank.

A number of administrators talked about taking risks and addressing failure. No one wants to fail, but failure is one of the best teachers for success. Thomas Edison, after thousands of false starts to discover a light bulb filament that would survive the heat of incandescence, stated that each time he tried a new filament and it failed, he was one step closer to what would work. Had each false step been recorded by Edison as a failure, perhaps he would have decided to stop his research and let people continue to burn oil for light; but he had the ability to face frustration, knowing that somewhere in his creative genius lay the answer to his problem.

Failure is a part of growing, but fear of failure and punishment for it are two sure ways to keep people from taking risks that could help an organization make giant leaps toward fulfilling its mission of service.

A superintendent in New Jersey stated that he received a number of honors for a variety of reasons, among them a willingness to take risks for children including being "in front" on a number of controversial issues such as funding, bilingual education, and the leadership role of the superintendency. The staff, parents, and board members told him that he listens, acts appropriately, cares for people, and makes decisions only with the interest of children as the top priority. They told him his leadership style included participatory decision making and a commitment to enable staff to grow professionally and as human beings. They told him he was a doer—a superb salesperson, open, honest—and an articulate spokesperson for public education.

Gale Gates (personal communication, March 9, 1991), a middle school principal in Louisiana, wrote:

> My philosophy has always been that as a school principal I manage people, not buildings. It is this style of management that I believe distinguishes me as an outstanding school administrator. I include teachers in making decisions, encourage new ideas and experimentation, and trust them to take risks. I offer them support for taking the initiative in developing their own leadership skills. Our school community is a "sharing" place with much emphasis on cooperation and collegiality. Many teachers have told me at one time or another, "I didn't think I could accomplish that but your encouragement and faith in me made me trust myself." My office door is always open to encourage communication and to share decision making.

Christa Metzger (personal communication, February 24, 1992), a superintendent in Arizona, shared her reason for being successful:

> There is another reason why I might be successful. I am willing to admit when I've made a mistake or don't know something. This frees others to risk doing something and not to be afraid to make mistakes. It generates a high level of activity and creativity in those around me because we're all on the same team—here to help each other succeed.

Amy Mook (personal communication, January 31, 1992), a high school principal in Minnesota, took a risk to improve graduation ceremonies. She states:

> Our graduation ceremonies used to be unruly, disrespectful, and bordering on a farce. I discussed the problem in our weekly principal's meeting. We decided the kids would be in charge of speakers, music, choosing K-12 staff as members of the honor guard, and so on. It has meant that one of the assistant principals and his secretary spend tons of time in the spring

working with the forty seniors nominated by staff. However, our graduation ceremonies have improved dramatically in the last decade as a result of listening to someone's ideas way back when and making the appropriate modifications.

These administrators all attribute their success to their willingness and ability to take calculated risks. In virtually every case, however, they stated clearly that their wanting to take risks was for the benefit of the students, staff, district, or community. Their mission was to serve the profession through improved learning opportunities for students and adults.

9

COMMUNICATION

"Communication is essential to the effective operation of any school" (Porod, 1993, 9). Can the importance of communication be stated more succinctly than that? Respondents of Project Success noted the importance of interactive communication and listening skills.

> I consider my communication skills to be the single most important aspect of my success as a high school principal. Whether I am dealing with faculty, students, parents, school board members, or other administrators, I must be able to express my views in clear, appropriate language. Often, I must attempt to persuade others to my point of view. The ability to respond to others in a sensitive fashion is critical to the effectiveness of a principal.
>
> I am very purposeful with all my communication. I am a good and attentive listener. (Wendel, Hoke, and Joekel, 1993b, 54)

The word *communication* is derived from a Latin word that means "common." The purpose of communication is to establish a common bond, a common understanding, or commonness, among persons. The establishment of commonness is based upon trust, mutual respect, frequent exchanges of ideas, and opportunities to engage in discussion of important matters, as one successful administrator noted. "I try to establish an atmosphere of trust and mutual respect with my faculty. We have regularly scheduled times when teachers can comfortably express their concerns and ideas, and have input into school decisions" (Joekel, Wendel, and Hoke, 1994, 35).

Two researchers found that communication skills were perceived as the most important set of skills among clarity of values and integrity, technical skills, creative ability, cultural sophistication, understanding of relevant issues, critical thinking skills, ability to learn from experience, respect for others, loyalty, foundational knowledge base, and specific knowledge base (Gousha and Mannan, 1991). Two elementary school administrators reiterated the primacy of communication: "No single skill is more important to a school leader than the ability to communicate effectively . . . . In large measure, good staff morale and positive parental support are built on communicating timely, accurate, and complete information" (Parish and Prager, 1992, 37). Effective communication comes through planning and conscious effort that solicits interactive, two-way communication.

In advice to new principals, Springston (1994) urged them to concentrate on four areas to be successful: organization, problem solving, discipline, and instructional leadership. In concluding remarks, he encouraged new principals to maintain open lines of communication.

> Communicate, communicate, communicate. New principals must be sure that open lines of communication are established in each of these categories at the beginning of the school year because communication is vital to so many aspects of the effective secondary school. I write a weekly memo to my staff members to advise them of all decisions made that may affect them and update them on coming events. (Springston, 1994, 29)

Now that the dawn of the information age is past, administrators must be prepared to communicate in more ways than ever before. The combination of new technology and expanded use of it in the public and private sectors, and in many homes as well, has provided more means of communication for administrators with their internal and external audiences. The expansion and proliferation of communication devices puts administrators into direct, instant contact with individuals through cellular phones, facsimile transmissions, electronic mail, voice mail, and other electronic forms of messaging. In addition, other improvements in communication have made communication with individuals and groups easier, more readily accessible, and more important. As a result, people expect to be kept informed because of the availability of technology and advancements in communication. The ease of desktop publishing has created greater expectations for school publications to be more attractive, letter perfect, and sophisticated in design. The presence in many homes of telephone answering machines increases the possibility of contacting parents, students, patrons, and other persons. Changes in society and the complexity of conditions amplify both the need for and the public's expectation of communication from school administrators.

DEFINITION

Communication is at the core of interpersonal and school-community relations. A major function of administrators is to inform their internal and external audiences and to obtain feedback from them about programs under their direction. The definition of the National School Public Relations Association (NSPRA) is as follows:

> Educational public relations is a planned and systematic two-way process of communication between an educational organization and its internal and external publics. Its program serves to stimulate a better understanding of the role, objectives, and accomplishments of the organization. Educational public relations is a management function which interprets public attitudes, identifies the policies and procedures of an individual organization with the public interest and executes a program of action to encourage public involvement and to earn public understanding and acceptance (NSPRA, 1972, 31).

Cleveland Hammonds (personal communication, March 11, 1992), a superintendent from Alabama, keyed upon the importance of communication to each individual in an organization.

> In my judgment, one of the most important functions of leadership is communication. As any leader views the people he or she wants to influence, it must be remembered that no one wants to be ignored or misunderstood. This challenges the leader to listen carefully and to seek interaction and response. The leader must hear, understand, and give effective feedback. It is essential that the leader project and communicate a sense of direction consistent with the data you have gotten from listening and other sources. If people see and hear parts of their ideas, hopes and aspirations in the operation or in future plans, there is that sense of ownership necessary to mobilize personnel and achieve the organization's goals.

Administrators are expected to be clear in their thoughts, lucid in their prose, open in their dialogue, and sensitive to the communication needs of their internal and external audiences. In addition, administrators must be technologically literate so they are expected to demonstrate technical expertise to an increasingly technologically literate society.

On the other hand, many individuals do not have access to sophisticated means of communication such as e-mail but lack basic devices such as a telephone or means of transportation to come to school for conferences. The communication needs of the poor are severe because of the limited means of interactive communication between administrators and family members. Consequently, administrators must make special efforts to communicate with audiences who have limited means of communication.

Communication needs of staff members vary by their positions, roles, need dispositions, and other factors. The authors of one study found that restructuring and teacher empowerment took place when principals shared information, opened lines of communication, and established rules on how to agree or disagree. "Teachers in the schools covered by the study report that they experienced the greatest sense of accomplishment when obstacles to communication were eliminated. In an atmosphere of open communication, these teachers felt that there was no decision too difficult to tackle" (Peel and Walker, 1994, 41-42).

Whether an audience is internal or external, linked to sophisticated communications or not, rich or poor, knowledgeable or uninformed about school programs, administrators must establish communication channels and eliminate obstacles to them. A principal from Hawaii explained how important communication was to success.

My function as an administrator has been to maintain a basic network of communication between elements of the school family . . . . I have always tried to be cognizant of the human factors in the learning organization. It is necessary to be human and also treat others with humanness. I have attempted to maintain an open ear and mind with all members of the school staff. Although it is impossible to satisfy everyone's demands, it is important to maintain a system of open communication, support the faculty and staff in their various endeavors, and strive to be honest and impartial.

CHANNELS OF COMMUNICATION

Administrators have at their disposal many means of communicating, beyond disseminating information (Costa, 1991). Among such means are bulletin and message boards, calendars, classroom observations, conferences, directories, handbooks, meetings, memos, newsletters, opinionnaires and surveys, person-to-person contacts, and walking about the school. Channels of communication and their utility may vary among internal groups (i.e., certified and noncertified staff) as well as among external audiences. Some staff members and students may pass several times daily by a bulletin board in a hallway, whereas others may rarely pass by the board. Some individuals rely heavily upon face-to-face contact, whereas others studiously devour written memos. Administrators need to reflect upon the needs of others as they consider the purpose of their message, how to deliver it, how to modify it for various audiences, and the possible impact it may have upon recipients; they must do likewise in considering how to solicit and receive feedback and how to follow up a message.

The greater the distance in time, space, frequency, and degree of interaction between administrators and others, the greater the difficulty in developing and maintaining effective communication. Regardless of the channel used to communicate to others, opportunities should be provided for interactive, two-way communication. Some communication is routine and affects only a few staff members, so posting a note to team members that a meeting will start a half hour later than usual is sufficient. Posting a note about some items, however, could set off a firestorm. Consider the outcomes of a memo posted on the last day of school, without any prior discussion or indication, stating that the teachers' lounge will be converted over the summer into a classroom for the ensuing school year.

In Oklahoma, an elementary school principal, Sandra Looper (personal communication, January 30, 1992), used tried-and-true channels of communication.

Although creating an atmosphere of trust, mutual respect, and collegiality seems like a relatively simple tenet, it is actually very complex and requires continual adaptation in order to be a vital component of school climate. Developing an ongoing system of communication is vital in order to establish rapport with teachers. Teachers are often so busy with their individual classroom responsibilities that unless the principal initiates a framework that allows teachers to work cooperatively as a team, then the opportunity for collegial situations may be stymied. Establishing regular faculty meetings where the total school staff can come together and discuss goals, problems, projects, and so on, is vital to the efficient functioning of a school. This helps the faculty to see the "whole picture" and to think in terms of continuity instead of just a segmented grade level. Although committees may have become a "dirty word" among educators, they do fulfill an important aspect of school planning. Teachers, parents, and administrators working together on curriculum concerns, schedules, budget priorities, and so on, provide a valuable service to their local schools. Each group brings its unique and sometimes divergent views to assist in making well-informed decisions regarding school programs . . . . Establishing an atmosphere of trust and mutual respect can also be assisted by providing regularly scheduled, small-group interaction times where teachers can comfortably express their concerns and ideas and have input to school decisions. Individual grade-level meetings allow teachers an informal format in which the principal has time to devote total concentration to the unique problems of a specific level. The intimacy of a small group also allows faculty to express concerns that may not be appropriate for a large-group setting. Having the opportunity to express ideas, concerns, and dreams welds the teachers and administrators together.

Communication with parents and guardians, service groups, and other external audiences requires much effort, planning, attention to detail, and preparation of content and method of delivery (McGough, 1990). For example, communicating to businesses and industry leaders that establishing school-business partnerships has reciprocal value will require precise analysis of the purpose, channels, and means of feedback over a long period. "Telling" members of the local chamber of commerce of the benefits of school-business partnerships is not likely to convince them of such benefits. Only when members of a chamber have had an opportunity to ask questions, consider the reciprocal value of partnerships, raise issues, reflect upon concerns, generate ideas, and weigh the concept in general and specific terms will leaders of businesses and industries be ready to commit themselves to school-business partnerships.

Because many stereotypes of schools and school programs exist, one of the primary objectives of communication is to change the way members of some groups see schools. The need to share views and to reach common understandings is basic to effective communication (Pankake, Stewart, and Winn, 1990).

GRAPEVINES

Announcements, information items, plans, requests for assistance, and other forms of communication flow through formal and informal channels—downward, upward, and laterally. In addition to official messages, other kinds of messages flow through informal networks, generally described as "grapevines." Unlike most means of communication based on formal organizational structures, grapevines are based on social relationships. Grapevines tend to form when employees want to share information that cannot be spread easily through formal channels, when formal channels restrict ease of communication, and when burning issues arise that affect employees' working conditions. Successful administrators recognize that grapevines can be useful means of communicating among employees and that they should seek to use them to their advantage.

One of the strengths of grapevines is that they are based on close personal relationships. News about personnel decisions, anticipated cutbacks in programs, and changes in organizational relationships, for example, can spread seemingly faster than the speed of sound or even the speed of light. An employee can overhear a conversation or catch a glimpse of a report and with one telephone call or conversation set in motion a chain of communication that permeates an entire organization within little time.

Although grapevines can carry unfounded rumors, most of the time the information they carry is accurate and timely (Davis, 1972). Because information is usually carried in predictable patterns, administrators can tap into grapevines and use them as positive means both to monitor traffic on them and to carry information.

Administrators can tap into grapevines by identifying key communicators such as department heads and secretaries, providing key information directly to them, and giving them the opportunity to spread such information face to face with members of their informal networks. Grapevines should not be used as substitutes for formal means of communication but should be recognized for the important part they play in inter- and intraorganizational communications (Wendel, 1980). Grapevines exist among external groups as well. Administrators who are alert to communication patterns identify key communicators in their communities and work with them to tap into concerns of community members and to engage key communicators in discussions of school-related issues. Members of clubs, businesses, civic associations, religious organizations, professions, and other groups can provide the names of persons who are influential and can serve as key communicators. An assistant superintendent from Nebraska noted that key communicators serve a vital function.

Communication is a critical ingredient for success. In order to be an effective communicator one must seek out audiences. For the school administrator this includes students, staff, parents, board members, state policy makers, and community. I believe in identifying key members of each group and maintaining constant communication. The purpose of the communication is to move the organization toward its goals.

Formal and informal conversations and discussions between school officials and key communicators can forge an effective communication chain to improve school-community relations. A high school principal from Delaware, Wayne Von Stetten, (personal communication, June 16, 1992), described how extensive efforts were required to dispel damaging rumors about his school.

During the years of the late 1960s and early into the 1970s, the drug scene was upon us almost in a flash, giving most school administrators little time to fend off this horrible blight. We never did dispose of the problem, of course, but we did manage to put to rest some of the irresponsible, false charges directed to us by uninformed members of the community. Rumors were rampant throughout the school community, and we found ourselves almost defenseless against the charges of widespread use of illegal drugs by students in classrooms, cafeteria, and so on. Letters disputing the false rumors failed to satisfy those who continued to charge us with operating a school that did little or nothing to curtail the use of drugs by students during the school day. The rumors were indeed spurious. We developed a plan that turned out to be the solution. I should mention that we always extended a general invitation to parents to visit the schools with few acceptances as did most administrations. And, of course, an unnatural "Back to School" evening, sponsored by the PTA, hardly gave parents an opportunity to see the school in operation—with students present! So we began to invite a cadre of parents to spend a full day with us, writing a personal letter to each of the twenty-five invited parents, asking them to the school to attend classes of their choice, eat in the cafeteria, converse with students and faculty, spend as much time as they like in our rest rooms, and playing fields. In other words, after an early morning bit of refreshments and a brief orientation, they were left "on their own" to see for themselves what the school's natural environment was all about. Out of the first batch of invitations sent, the response was an overwhelming twenty-two acceptances. Within one school year, we had 200 parents spend a full day with us, with a whopping 90 percent acceptance rate . . . the day was unstructured in every sense.

The outcome of this program, which we called Parent Visitation Day (PVD), was the accumulation of literally hundreds of disciples for the school. Those who saw firsthand what the school was about, as a result of having spent a full day with us, were some of our strongest supporters. They were able to diffuse some of the erroneous rumors about the school by simply saying, "That's not true—I should know, for I spent a full day at the school." We received numerous letters from the participants, all exclaiming their pleasure with our PVD program; there were also invitations sent to those whom we could identify as perpetrators of the rumor mills, with the result that we were able to convince them that the school was indeed a place where teaching and learning were taking place in an atmosphere completely unlike the scene they were describing to fellow citizens. Some of our original severe critics became our staunchest supporters.

HOSTILE ENVIRONMENTS

Exchanges in hostile environments tax administrators' skills in oral and nonverbal communication, stress tolerance, conflict resolution, and sensitivity. Disruptive, rude, angry, fearful, or frustrated students, parents, teachers, manipulators, intimidators, and others with unresolved problems create demanding situations for administrators, who often face confrontations without warning. Conditions in the United States comprise a fertile field for problems to sprout (Zill and Nord, 1994).

A superintendent in Delaware related a favorite story about a telephone call from a hostile parent.

One afternoon at approximately 4:00 P.M. I received a telephone call from a mother who wanted to know who was the "stupid jerk" who made the decision not to close school earlier because of the snow storm. I told her that I was the one who made and took full responsibility for the decision and further that I had made an error in not realizing earlier the severity of the storm. I assured her that all building principals, transportation personnel, and I would not leave to go home until we had confirmation that all students had arrived home safely. This did not seem to satisfy her, and she kept the conversation going for approximately thirty minutes, advising me in the utmost detail how the situation should have been handled with "I hope you don't make the same stupid mistake tomorrow!" I replied, "I do not intend to. If you will give me your telephone number, I will call you at 5:00 A.M. tomorrow and allow you to make the decision." She hastily indicated she did not want that responsibility. We had a good laugh. The entire conversation was positive, since although she was upset, I recognized the reason for her anxiety and was able to put everything into perspective with a "sense of humor."

What administrators say initially in hostile environments can defuse or add fire to smoldering or flaming situations. A good first rule to follow is to refuse to fight. Replies to persons who are upset should be spoken calmly, in a pleasant tone, at a moderate rate, with low volume, clearly phrased, and in a noninflammatory, poised manner. Sensitivity to individuals can be shown by asking them to describe their problems at the outset. The time taken to describe problems can create a buffer zone or a cooling down period.

Some techniques to create a buffer zone before having to confront irate individuals are to have a secretary delay face-to-face meetings by (1) screening telephone calls, writing down the nature of complaints, and thus having administrators return calls forewarned; (2) asking persons in the office to fill out a short "complaint" form for administrators to peruse before meeting the persons, or (3) asking complainants for information and telling them, "Please wait just a minute," before informing the administrator of the situation and ushering them into an administrator's office (Solomon, 1990).

DIRECTED LISTENING

Showing sensitivity to needs and concerns of others is necessary in all situations and is particularly valuable in hostile environments. The degree of sensitivity to individuals' needs and concerns can be increased by what one says after others' comments. Nelson and Heeney (1984) advocated an approach they called directed listening: Listen by giving nonverbal clues of attention such as nodding. Clarify by asking for clarification or rephrase thoughts and ideas. Encourage by asking relevant questions about the problem. Comment by presenting objective perceptions and adding information. Focus by restating the problem. Explore alternative solutions by negotiating and evaluate alternative solutions. Demonstrate by giving examples of what might be done. Direct by identifying specific courses of short- and long-range actions, and reinforce by outlining factors for positive conditions.

An assistant superintendent from Missouri described the value derived from listening to what others have to say through formal committees.

> My method of seeking input from others is that I take time to listen and share with teachers. A good example of this is my method of interaction with the curriculum and policies committee. I make sure that all committee members have a chance to voice their opinions and I listen intently. On issues affecting the school I ask each one to honestly share his or her thoughts with the rest of the committee. This way all issues and opinions are communicated . . . . I enjoy working with students and I interact frequently with them. Opinions are gained through administrative advisory committees and parent and student advisory committees. It is an interactive process in which I take time to listen to each person's opinion.

In Missouri, a high school principal was a value-added listener, as he perceived that others' ideas are expressions of their dreams. "I enjoy assisting people set and reach dreams. I get equally excited when that happens with adolescents or adults. People are full of dreams; yet most are unaware of their power to make them happen. I am an excellent listener, and I use that to find the right ways to empower individuals to seek their dreams."

Gerald Freitag (personal communication, March 10, 1992), a central office administrator in Wisconsin, indicated that the magic in listening is internalizing what others have said so that their meaning becomes clear.

> After pondering the question regarding my success, I have no earth-shattering revelations. Many of the factors I believe play a significant role in determining one's success are commonplace. They include attributes all prospective administrators have to varying degrees. The real catalyst is how one utilizes these attributes in practice. In my estimation, the key ingredients are the common people skills. You have to be an active listener who is willing to spend the time with staff, students, parents, and citizens. The administrator must really hear what is being said and utilize all sources of input to formulate a final position.

SENSITIVITY AND STRESS TOLERANCE

Administrators need to have the ability to think on their feet in stressful situations, to select appropriate words and phrases whether writing or speaking, to be diplomatic and tactful, and to project a desire for harmonious relations. They must also be decisive, willing to assume responsibility, persuasive, and able to avoid negative behaviors such as arrogance (Hersey and Blanchard, 1988). In stressful situations, administrators must have the poise to remain in charge of their emotions and to build bridges of understanding.

MULTICULTURAL ISSUES

Communicating with persons from other countries and with different cultures poses particular issues (Yao, 1988). Body distance, eye contact, gestures, the importance of saving face, word choice, such as using "reserved" rather than "passive," pressure upon children to do well in school, and other factors affect communication among peoples of different cultures and thus affect subsequent understanding and cooperation between administrators and their clients who may hail from different backgrounds. Administrators need to pay even greater attention to their words and body language in communicating with individuals from other cultures so that their intent and meaning are neither improperly communicated nor misinterpreted.

Cross-cultural communication is increasing in importance as more and more students in schools are not native born Americans. Language barriers come readily to mind, and they may be even greater for students from some Southeast Asian countries who have little exposure to written language until they enter the United States. Asians and Pacific Islanders (APIs) have different views toward social institutions as schools. Teachers are respected as professionals who have authority over children, and APIs believe that they should not interfere with schooling. Administrators and teachers who seek to involve APIs in school programs may thus be viewed as incompetent and unable to decide matters for themselves. Because of such a cultural difference, administrators and teachers must explain to APIs that parent involvement is not a sign of weakness and indecisiveness but considered an essential element in home-school relations (NSPRA, 1993).

Many APIs place a high value upon formal education, and their children's success or failure in school reflects upon family integrity and honor. Consequently, children from API families may suffer from anxiety over grades and tests, social isolation from peers who are less concerned about their performance in school, and lowered self-esteem when performance in school does not match their families' expectation (Shen and Mo, 1990). The views of APIs about psychological stress in children can be another source of concern, as APIs may believe that such stress is a result of physical illness or a lack of motivation and brings shame upon the family (Kleinman and Good, 1985). APIs may have difficulty in understanding concepts such as learning disabilities that explain children's learning difficulties.

Other cultural differences may exist about time; for example, some Southeast Asians believe that time is a better problem solver than actions by persons; their seeming reluctance to "do something" to help their children or to show up punctually for meetings is not indifference but a reflection of a different belief about time. Furthermore, in conversations about problems, APIs may seem polite but suddenly erupt in anger. Their anger may be aroused because their body language was not noticed and the nonverbal cues they sent were ignored by administrators or teachers. Head nodding, smiles, and verbal agreement by APIs do not necessarily indicate full agreement with the ideas, plans, and views of school officials. Thus administrators must make concerted efforts to understand others' cultures to communicate effectively with them.

NONVERBAL COMMUNICATION

"Actions speak louder than words." So can gestures, body language, facial expressions, dress, ways of greeting persons and seating them, and other nonverbal forms of communication that account for some 55 percent of interpersonal communication. Distinctions may be made between nonverbal behavior, or conduct, demeanor, and way of action; and (2) nonverbal communication, or ways of sending, giving, or transmitting information. The effects of smiling, maintaining eye contact, dressing professionally, sitting alongside persons rather than behind a desk, and related aspects have a bearing upon how administrators' words and intentions are perceived by others (Loccisano, 1992).

DESIGNING FORMAL COMMUNICATIONS

What characteristics of formal communications, oral and written, grab your interest? Keep them in mind as you prepare notes for speeches and written materials such as reports, memos, and letters.

First, clarify the purpose of your communication because it will affect the tone, approach, and style you will use. Is your purpose related to details of a program or event, the "big picture," or to both? Choose an approach that matches your purpose with your audience's probable degree of interest. You cannot expect that what is important to you will be important to members of your intended audience. Seek to capture the interest of your audience at the opening of your message.

Second, prepare an outline and work from it as you prepare your report, letter, memo, newsletter, or talk. The act of preparing an outline will help you order your thoughts, develop your theme, tie ideas together, and consider the main parts of your message—opening, main points, and closing.

Third, consider the nature of your audience. The members of some groups may be unfamiliar with educational terms and jargon, not accustomed to reading technical language, or confused by long, rambling sentences. In some cases, you may need to rewrite a message for different audiences. For example, newsletters to parents of non-English-speaking students may have to be rewritten, at least in part, rather than translated word for word.

Communications should seek to satisfy the unmet needs of receivers. Intended receivers who do not recognize that they have a need or deny a need for communications from school administrators pose particular challenges for the senders of messages.

Fourth, revise, clarify, shorten, rewrite. Cull unnecessary material, such as background information that clutters or obscures the intended message. Place key points at the beginning of your communication rather than bury the heart of a message deep within a text or speech. Remember, your purpose is to inform the reader or listener. Your language must be concise and clear.

Last, check everything several times. Look up the meaning of words, their spelling, and their usage; for example, *inservice* is an adjective, not a verb or noun. Ask colleagues to review your notes or written material and listen to their suggestions. If you are delivering a talk, check pronunciation of words and practice your talk so that you are not a prisoner of your written notes.

Once a message is sent, the words and their meaning cannot be recalled. Apologies, explanations, clarification, and other efforts to correct what was written or said may be made, but the original message remains. Say what you mean and mean what you say.

SENDING FORMAL COMMUNICATIONS

Written communications can be sent in memos to internal audiences, business letters, thank-you notes, newsletters, reports, proposals, bulletin board pinups, handbooks, and rules and regulations. The nature of each written communication dictates the style that is used; letters to parents or business leaders are in a form distinct from that used in memos to staff members. The style and approach to writing material for a student handbook provides a clue to the climate of the school, how students and their behaviors are viewed, and possibly how students are expected to behave. Each written communication should be examined solely to measure the match of the message with its style.

Reports to target audiences convey as much about the writer as they do about the content of the report. Compare the preparation of a report to your board of education about the language arts program in your school with one to the faculty on plans for the preschool orientation next summer. The purpose, audience, and interest in the message of each report should determine how each is drafted.

Classification of Messages

Communications to internal audiences can be classified as (1) informative, or messages about functions, programs, services, and tasks; (2) innovative, or messages about new approaches, ideas, and technology; (3) integrative, or messages about relationships among individuals with organizational goals, expectations, and needs; and (4) regulative, or messages about policies, rules, and regulations (Morley and Shockley-Zalabak, 1986). Factor in whether a message is to be drafted to superordinates, peers, or subordinates, and immediately other considerations come to mind. Compare how an innovative message might be drafted to one's superordinate asking for additional funding for a new program, to one's peers asking for their support for the new program that might diminish the allocation of resources to their needs, or to one's subordinates asking for their willingness to adopt the program.

One important responsibility of administrators is to disseminate integrative messages about organizational expectations of staff members or to communicate social controls (Gougeon, Hutton, and McPherson, 1990). How do teachers, for example, react to social control communications? Gougeon and his associates found that teachers rated principals lower than principals rated themselves in the use of social control communications. The perceptions of teachers about social control communications of principals were correlated to three factors: the degree of closeness the teachers felt to their principals, the teachers' perceptions of the frequency of their interactions with their principals, and the teachers' perceptions of the visibility of their principals in their schools. The import of those findings is that effective communication does not occur in a vacuum and that communication is built upon trust, openness, frequency of contacts, and other interpersonal factors.

Teachers' needs for feedback, reward, motivation, and support are tied directly to communication with administrators (Whaley, 1994). Communication between administrators and all staff members is essential for job satisfaction, development of staff, site-based management, and school improvement.

ORAL COMMUNICATIONS

Administrators deliver hundreds of oral communications daily ranging from brief instructions to a secretary about drafting a letter to a supplier about damaged goods to formal presentations to civic groups. How administrators deliver their messages is as important as what they say. The human voice can be an effective tool, and the subtleties of enunciation, modulation, pronunciation, pitch, rate, tone, and volume provide valuable means of adding emphasis, meaning, and intent to messages.

Likewise, skill in delivering a message can be enhanced through presenting ideas and thoughts logically, having effective opening and closing statements, using audiovisual methods and materials, being enthusiastic, maintaining eye contact, avoiding the use of linguistic nonfluencies, establishing good rapport, using appropriate gestures and facial expressions, and making good use of time.

Communication can be enhanced by using both oral and written approaches. A memo placed in staff members' mailboxes about an issue deemed crucial to an administrator may not be viewed as such without follow-up actions, such as person-to-person conversations, small-group meetings, and other kinds of formal and informal meetings. Whereas words in a written memo may indicate that an issue is critical, follow-up actions to a memo amplify, clarify, and reinforce the urgency of the matter.

WRITTEN COMMUNICATIONS

The purpose of writing is to inform readers. A useful written communication contains a worthwhile message that is clearly and concisely stated. Effective writers engage readers' interest at the outset, present their main ideas logically and sequentially, and offer examples, illustrations, or other means to clarify their main ideas. Effective writers use action verbs rather than the passive voice; for example, Julius Caesar said, "I came. I saw. I conquered," rather than "The place has been visited by me and has been conquered by me." Caesar's crisp phrasing pounds home the intensity of his actions.

The subjects in paragraphs and sentences should be clear and guide readers to follow the theme in the communication. Short paragraphs and sentences are easy to follow and to comprehend. Simple words should be used; for example, *used* is a better choice than *utilized*.

In the preparation of written communications, several points should be kept in mind:

1. the purpose of the message
2. the background and conditions relevant to the message
3. the recipients' knowledge of and attitudes toward the message
4. the main ideas to be presented
5. a way to organize the main points of the message

6. a way to open the message so that it attracts interest

7. a way to end the message so that readers grasp the main points

Materials can be planned for three kinds of readers—thirty-second, three-minute, and thirty-minute. The first, those who might devote only thirty seconds to a memo or letter, must be captivated into reading the entire material, or at least a major portion of it, with attention-grabbing features. A three-minute reader will likely look for headlines, headings and subheadings, and the main point at the beginning. Those who may devote more attention—the thirty-minute readers— deserve equal consideration and should receive well-written material even though they comprise the minority of readers.

LISTENING AND SENSITIVITY

I know you believe you understand what you think I said, but I am not sure you realize that what you heard is not what I meant.

Anonymous

Listening is a separate skill from oral and written communication. Some individuals have excellent skills in oral communication but may have poor skills in written communication, and vice versa. Likewise, individuals may have excellent skills in oral communication but poor listening skills and poor sensitivity to the needs and concerns of others. Some persons may have excellent skills in written communication but little ability to grasp the meaning of others' written messages and similarly lack sensitivity to the needs and concerns of others. An administrator from Rhode Island succinctly noted that the key to being a successful superintendent is "the ability to listen, and more importantly, to hear what students, parents, teachers, and the community are saying, is paramount to success."

Administrators who have poor listening skills and lack sensitivity diminish the value of their interactions with others, get little benefit from comments and feedback in conversations, fail to interpret others' meaning in their responses, and as a result thwart interactive communication. Likewise, administrators with little ability to identify others' needs and concerns in written messages erase the value of such messages by failing to grasp their intent.

Successful administrators intellectually absorb the context, words, images, intent, and implications conveyed in messages to them. They can enhance listening skills through conscious acts such as preparing to listen by focusing attention upon others who are talking; concentrating upon other people's words, ideas, and body language so that distracters are eliminated; being attentive to verbal and nonverbal clues; seeking to gain understanding of what others say, for example, by asking for clarification, probing for more information, or being patient and letting others speak without interrupting them; checking the accuracy of others' ideas by restating their thoughts and seeking affirmation of inferences or by acknowledging how others feel; and giving feedback in verbal and nonverbal ways so that others know their messages are received.

Some bad listening habits to avoid are deeming a speaker's subject uninteresting, pretending to be listening to a speaker, being negative about a speaker's presentation skills, and putting too much emphasis on one comment. Letting value-laden words trigger personal animosities, daydreaming, focusing attention upon other matters, noting facts to the exclusion of intent, and ignoring problems and concerns are other bad listening habits to avoid. Listeners should monitor their habits so that their listening skills improve. One simple means, of course, is to repeat what a speaker has said so that both the intent and the key concepts of a speaker's message are received.

The ear may hear spoken words of others, but only the mind may receive the message in spoken words. Effective listeners, first of all, do just that—listen. The temptation to talk, above all, should be resisted so that the feelings, ideas, implications, and intent of others are received. After a few interruptions, rebuttals, denials, and other rejections, speakers may simply decide that their message will not be received and quit talking. Nonperceptive receivers may thus conclude that speakers did not really have much to say and thus would have missed the whole point of the messages that were aborted.

Successful administrators are sensitive to the written words of others. Persons who take the time to prepare written communications expect the receivers of their messages to read and react to them. The needs and concerns in written messages can be addressed through careful analysis of the words and phrases in them and by conversations afterward to confirm or to gain further information from written messages. Much information can be gained from senders, and their communications should be analyzed carefully lest important concepts, concerns, and needs be overlooked.

EVALUATING COMMUNICATIONS

How do you analyze your success in using communication channels? in oral communications? in written communications? in formal communications? in informal communications? in nonverbal communications? in internal and external grapevines? To whom do you turn for feedback? How do you obtain feedback? How do you incorporate feedback into self-development?

Rating scales, self-assessment techniques, surveys, opinionnaires, interviews by telephone, and other kinds of instruments and procedures can be used to gather information about communication skills and to assess human realities in schools (Tewel, 1990). Information may be gathered about communications with certified and noncertified staff, students, peers, parents and guardians, key communicators, patrons, members of community groups, members of the media, leaders of civic and governmental organizations, and selected target audiences. Data may also be gathered about academic and co-curricular programs, school-community relations, school operations, and other aspects of the organization and administration of schools.

Barriers to written and oral communication skills can and should be examined because of their importance in transmitting a school's purposes, goals, and achievements. Podsen (1991) developed a measure of writing apprehension, the Principal's Writing Inventory (PWI), on job-related writing tasks of school principals. Administrators may wish to consider the PWI and other means of analyzing and improving their skills in written and oral communication. Hartzell and Nelson (1994), for example, established criteria for writing effective letters of recommendation, and Kindred, Bagin, and Gallagher (1984) have numerous suggestions for improving oral communication to groups such as smile, speak to individuals, be sincere, and eliminate voice and diction distracters and annoying mannerisms. Their suggestions could be adapted to make self-analyses and to obtain feedback from colleagues and members of audiences.

Often, school-community relations is considered a separate program, something not requiring administrators' personal communication skills. Oral and written communication skills are tools for conveying the mission, goals, and achievements of the school, its staff, and students. Building and maintaining good school-community relationships may be premised on the concept that the school and community share responsibility for education. Further, building and maintaining good school-community relationships remains a primary responsibility of educators. "The key to sound relationships is development of the idea that education is the job of all citizens. In achieving this, educators must take the public into partnership, using wisely the tools of persuasion, information, and cooperation. Responsibility rests primarily with the educator" (Cutlip and Center, 1971, 562).

School-community relations programs may be analyzed separately and formally. Van Meter (1993) outlined a one-day workshop for analyzing existing school-community activities and for exploring options. Other avenues may be developed for evaluating features of a school's communication programs, activities, and system.

Much like setting up any plan, administrators who are interested in evaluating their communications will establish a purpose, identify questions to be answered, identify data sources, collect information from such sources, analyze the information once it is collected, reach conclusions, and act upon the information. Setting up a team to evaluate communications should result in an evaluation program that is broad in scope. Evaluation programs should be designed to be continuous and comprehensive, comprised of formative and summative stages, with feedback loops built into each step or process of evaluation. Procedures and plans for improving communication should be based upon results from analysis of data. Administrators who demonstrate their willingness to improve their communication skills will reinforce the trust and mutual respect they have built with members of their school and community.

SUMMARY

Communication is both a means to build organizational relationships and a function of organizational relationships. Successful administrators will find and use means of communication to build close relationships with others and to capitalize upon those relationships by extending communication patterns, increasing the depth of understanding with others, and sharpening their means of oral and written communication. Administrators who are effective communicators value the ideas of and feedback from others and also seek to improve their listening skills.

REFERENCES

Costa, E. (1991). How to communicate with your community: 25 tips. *NASSP Bulletin, 75* (537), 124-126.

Cutlip, S. M., & Center, A. H. (1971). *Effective public relations* (4th ed.). Englewood Cliffs, NJ: Prentice-Hall.

Davis, K. (1972). *Human behavior at work*. New York: McGraw-Hill.

Gougeon, T. D., Hutton, S. I., & McPherson, J. L. (1990, April). *A quantitative phenomenological study of leadership: Social control theory applied to actions of school principals*. Paper presented at the annual meeting of the American Educational Research Association, Boston, MA.

Gousha, R. P., & Mannan, G. (1991). *Analysis of selected competencies: Components, acquisition and measurement perceptions of three groups of stakeholders in education*. Paper presented at the annual meeting of the National Conference of Professors of Educational Administration, Fargo, ND. (ERIC Document Reproduction Service No. 336 850).

Hartzell, G. N., & Nelson, K. (1994). How to write an effective letter. *The High School Magazine, 1*(3), 35-38.

Hersey, P., & Blanchard, K. (1988). *Management of organizational behavior*. Englewood Cliffs, NJ: Prentice-Hall.

Joekel, R. G., Wendel, F. C., & Hoke, F A. (1994). Principals can make a difference. *Principal, 73*(4), 34-36.

Kindred, L. W., Bagin, D., & Gallagher, D. R. (1984). Making oral presentations. In *The school & community relations* (3rd ed.). Englewood Cliffs, NJ: Prentice-Hall.

Kleinman, A., & Good, B. J. (1985). *Culture and depression*. Berkeley: University of California Press.

Loccisano, J. F. (1992). *Nonverbal communication and its implications for school personnel: A literature review*. (ERIC Document Reproduction Service No. ED 352 697).

McGough, M. R. (1990). Increased communication lessens confrontation. *NASSP Bulletin, 74*(527), 132-134.

Morley, D. D., & Shockley-Zalabak, P. (1986). Conflict avoiders and compromisers: Toward an understanding of the organizational communication style. *Group & Organization Studies, 11*(4), 387-402.

National School Public Relations Association. (1972). *Evaluation instrument for educational public relations programs.* Arlington, VA: Author.

National School Public Relations Association. (1993). *Capturing the best of the 1993 NSPRA seminar.* Arlington, VA: Author.

Nelson, D., & Heeney, W. (1984). Directed listening: A model for improved administrative communication. *NASSP Bulletin, 68*(472), 124-129.

Pankake, A. M., Stewart, G. K., & Winn, W. (1990). Choices for effective communication: Which channels to use? *NASSP Bulletin, 74*(529), 53-57.

Parish, J., & Prager, D. (1992). Communication: The key to effective leadership. *Principal, 72*(1), 37-39.

Peel, H. A., & Walker, B. L. (1994). What it takes to be an empowering principal. *Principal, 73*(4), 41-42.

Podsen, I. J. (1991). Apprehension and effective writing in the principalship. *NASSP Bulletin, 75*(532), 89-96.

Porod, G. N. (1993). New roles for teachers. *Schools in the Middle, 3*(2), 7-10.

Shen, W., & Mo, W. (1990). *Reaching out to their cultures: Building communication with Asian American families.* (Eric Document Reproduction Service No. 351 435).

Solomon, M. (1990). *Working with difficult people.* Englewood Cliffs, NJ: Prentice-Hall.

Springston, J. (1994). Four areas of communication. *The High School Magazine, 2*(1), 29.

Tewel, K. J. (1990). Improving in-school communications: A technique for principals. *NASSP Bulletin, 74*(524), 39-41.

Van Meter, E. J. (1993). Setting new priorities: Enhancing the school-community relations program. *NASSP Bulletin, 77*(554), 22-27.

Wendel, F. C. (1980). The communication grapevine. In *The public relations almanac for educators.* Camp Hill, PA: Educational Communication Center.

Wendel, F. C., Hoke, F. A., & Joekel, R. G. (1993b). Project success: Outstanding principals speak out. *The Clearing House, 67*(1), 52-54.

Whaley, K. W. (1994). Leadership and teacher job satisfaction. *NASSP Bulletin, 78*(564), 46-50.

Yao, E. L. (1988). Working effectively with Asian immigrant parents. *Phi Delta Kappan, 70*(3), 223-225.

Zill, N., & Nord, C. W. (1994). *Running in place: How American families are faring in a changing economy and an individualistic society.* Washington, DC: Child Trends.

10

SELECTION

Those administrators nominated for this study who attributed their success to their ability to select superior people discussed the importance of hiring and working with professionals who exhibited characteristics analogous to those demonstrated by the most successful administrators in the profession. They also appreciated being selected for this study because of their competence.

Webster's defines *select* as "chosen from a number or group by fitness or preference; of special value or excellence." (*Webster's Ninth New Collegiate Dictionary*, 1990). Outstanding administrators said it is possible to differentiate among individuals who exhibit talents and proclivities for a particular educational position. Subsequently, administrators said they surround themselves with the most talented people they can select. Why is surrounding oneself with talented people so important? A number of administrators said it provided them a unique freedom when working with the most talented people. That freedom came from being able to work with the capable individuals rather than to spend time monitoring their activities to help improve performance.

Highly talented people have more freedom and mental energy to apply their competence to the improvement of their performance knowing that to do so is in line with the underlying reason they were selected in the first place. They create an atmosphere of challenge, of competence, of increased efforts to achieve, to help, to encourage, to succeed. This energy is a stimulant to others who feel encouraged to put forth their best efforts. Talented people know they have an obligation to support the efforts of others. If these efforts are less than successful, they do not condemn; they teach, they coach, they support, they console. They devote time and energy to looking for ways others can contribute their best efforts while still working to develop more capability and effectiveness for the good of the system.

Talented people are closer to knowing and demonstrating the upper reaches of their potential. Others may not work as they do, think as they do, or accomplish as much as they do; but they know talented individuals are making unique contributions to the system. It is more important to support and utilize talent than it is to be concerned whether or not that talent is similar. Talented people know others are watching them work and lead. In many cases, others are trying to imitate their actions and style to increase their own accomplishments. To the talented, challenges provide opportunities, opportunities provide solutions, solutions provide affirmation, and affirmations provide freedom.

Why would a successful administrator even consider selecting any but the very best people? The potential cost to an organization for hiring less than the best is enormous. The professional time to monitor and coach these individuals, the legal costs, the wasted salary and benefits, not to mention the damage done to the organization, all point to the importance of hiring the very best. The entire organization benefits from the hiring of superior people.

A school district's investment in a single professional can easily exceed $30,000 per year. If a mediocre professional were to be retained for ten years, the cost to the district would be $300,000 not to mention loss in reduced learning and performance by the students under the tutelage of this individual. All school boards must hire the very best candidates for all professional and support positions.

The best professionals talk about wanting to be around people with fresh ideas. They want to be involved in formulating change to improve the district. They take their work seriously and continually look for ways to improve their administration and their effect on the lives of students and adults. They provide candid appraisals of current policy and are ready to offer positive suggestions for continuous improvements.

Wayne Haver (personal communication, April 20, 1992), a high school principal in Arkansas, wrote:

> I am successful because I have surrounded myself with a strong staff and have given them the freedom to be innovative, to utilize their skills, and to develop their programs to the fullest. I see my responsibility as providing an atmosphere conducive to learning along with the materials and equipment necessary for the staff to perform their jobs at the highest level possible. The ability to motivate people and to establish a positive approach to life has helped me to be successful. I have set high expectations for myself, the staff, and our students. I communicate those, enforce them, and reward them.

A high school principal in Georgia said it was simple for him to summarize why he had been recognized for success in school administration: He was able to surround himself with good people who had a genuine commitment to excellence. He believed it was his roll to serve as a facilitator. He tried to enable capable individuals to be the best they could be by providing them the tools needed for success (and those tools vary with every individual).

A high school principal in Hawaii said the talent she possessed was the ability to recognize talent in others and to match needs with resources. Also, she had been willing to recognize where she fell short and was able to build complementary relationships within the school to compensate. Her nature was to look within herself for solutions, but she strived to keep current and to be creative in utilizing information in school improvement efforts. She generally saw challenges instead of problems. She firmly believed that in life people will find whatever it is they look for. She always looks for the positive and best in people and situations and has always been surrounded by wonderful students and teachers.

A high school principal in Missouri was complimented on his leadership abilities. A veteran teacher once remarked that his best quality was that he hired the best teachers he could find and then "got the hell out of the way" and let them do their jobs.

A Georgia high school principal identified another strength of administrators who pride themselves on hiring superior people. To be a successful school administrator, she hired competent employees and then recognized and utilized the strengths of each.

A high school principal in Iowa wrote that he supports and encourages his good people. He felt he had the ability to judge the character and quality people possess and place them in positions where they will be most effective. As a principal, he considers it his job to hire good people, support them, and give them the encouragement to do the job they were hired to do in the manner that seems most comfortable and effective.

A superintendent in Virginia, picks the very best available people for jobs and gives them freedom and flexibility in performing their tasks.

Why do these administrators give so much latitude to the professionals who work for them? As many of them said, they know the capabilities of the individuals. Give those professionals the opportunity to think for themselves, to design strategies, and to implement procedures that benefit the students, the schools, and the districts. Successful administrators who hire outstanding people encourage them to make decisions as one of the team members.

John Prasch (personal communication, November 1991), a retired superintendent in Nebraska, responded philosophically when asked about his ability to hire outstanding staff members. "[I have] the ability to surround myself with able colleagues and to work with them on a nonjudgmental basis. I never assumed my role was to supervise or to direct but thought it more appropriate to coordinate and facilitate the development of others."

Administrators were not shy about discussing the fact that the students are the primary audience for which excellent staff are being hired. A superintendent in Minnesota, for example, talked about the match between outstanding teachers and the students. He placed a priority on hiring good people. He wanted people who like what they were doing and who liked kids or understood that kids were the main target. He wanted professionals with enthusiasm, commitment, and a willingness to examine better ways to do things.

Are these administrators the kinds of people who can make a positive impact? Are these the people who hire the outstanding teachers, those who in turn inspire students to make their best efforts? Are these the people who will invest themselves in a commitment to positive improvements in students and adults? You bet they are!

After twenty-seven years in the school business and with documented success and awards, Don Gray (personal communication), a junior high school principal in Missouri, gives a recipe for recruiting and hiring quality staff:

- Involve teaching staff in the hiring process (allow department with the opening to interview and listen to the applicants).
- Check your applicants in every way possible. (I sometimes call back to their last two principals to make sure of the recommendation.)
- Allow candidates to substitute teach if possible to get a feel for the school.
- Make the candidates aware of the school philosophy to determine if it matches their philosophy.
- Build a school with such a reputation for excellence that the best teachers in the district want to work there and ask to transfer.
- Work with the personnel director to make sure he or she understands what you are looking for in a middle-level educator.

He explains: I'm really not sure the above is all that unique. I am sure it works, however, and am blessed with a wonderful group of people who care about kids. They make our school work and deserve the credit. The secret to good school administration is surrounding yourself with quality people. This junior high school has such people, and this is a great place to learn.

An important way to ensure that a district continues to hire the best people is for the board of education to approve a written policy stating its intent to hire only the most competent personnel. This, however, is easy to do but difficult to implement. In too many districts, the temptation is to hire the next in line, the faithful or even the moderately successful employee, although not necessarily the most outstanding. These hiring practices are often implemented under the guise of helping maintain morale, but what has been the effect on those professionals who know they are superior employees and who now see the district hiring mediocre professionals to maintain harmony?

In many districts entrenched employees will see to it that the mediocre are left alone. For the board to set a policy to hire and promote only the best can cause a real-life crises that will have to be faced. The price tag for hiring less than the best employees is more than the average district can afford. Strapped for money, many districts stress the short-term economic necessity to hire many new professionals, since they do not command the higher salaries and benefits. This false economy may be played out later with lost opportunities by hundreds of students who could have been inspired and motivated by a professional who excited and challenged their desire to excel.

Unfortunately, some districts even make sure these less-seasoned teachers do not receive tenure so the district can continue to hire the least expensive teachers. Is this the same district that wants to keep high morale? Is this the district whose actions speak louder than words? Is this the school district whose board members were elected to provide the very best educational system possible with the resources available?

Many districts today are using some form of structured interview in their hiring procedures. This interview technique provides an opportunity for each candidate to be asked exactly the same questions. A trained professional scores the responses to correlate conceptual and behavioral responses with responses discussed by the very best professionals.

A trained professional not only can predict the likelihood of success by the candidates but also can use the same interview materials to build a developmental profile providing suggestions for professional development to improve areas of vuinerability.

If a district uses the more sophisticated instruments available to sort and rank talent, and is careful not to interfere with the process, this district should, over time, outperform other districts not using a similar, objective selection technique.

So why would a district not use a comprehensive system to identify the best talent? Sometimes local politics gets in the way. At other times, those who need to make the final decision will interject their own biases to the detriment of the objective system. Those with wider vision, the readers of this book perhaps, will: (1) check to see what selection system is being used by the district, (2) insist that the best system be implemented, (3) continue to monitor the selections to support hiring the best candidates, and (4) be sure everyone knows and supports the efforts of the board to continue this policy.

If the district does not have a policy or does not have trained interviewers among the administrators, encourage the board to identify individuals for certified training. Also encourage the establishment of a hiring process that gives building-level principals greater responsibility for interviewing and selecting superior people. When the principal has this responsibility, he or she will be more inclined to hire the best, since ultimately the success of the school is the principal's direct responsibility. Outstanding administrators felt they should be responsible for making the final decisions about new employees, but they were specific in wanting to maintain a system that gave others in the organization a chance to be involved in the selection process.

Where principals were responsible for the selection of teachers and support personal, they wanted others in the building to have the chance to review and interview candidates. Obviously, most of this concern centered around trying to match the personalities of the instructional and support team. However, this did not dissuade the best administrators from hiring the best candidates. In most cases, the best candidates have versatile human relations skills and make definite overtures to get along with their potential workmates.

When principals are held responsible for the total results of their schools and the professionals in them, we find these administrators much more likely to want to have the final word on hiring. In a number of cases, they even wanted to have the opportunity to challenge the selection of the superintendent if they felt the teacher candidate was not the best choice. Since excellent administrators spend a great deal of time with the professional staff, they want to hire someone who is versatile, is competent, and has a proclivity for progress within the school setting.

In a number of cases, administrators described interviewing committees that met with the eligible candidates. Although they did not elaborate on the types of questions being asked, they did describe a process that helped the veteran teachers get a good sense of the relative competence of the candidate. They asked candidates to share their mission, objectives, and philosophy as it related to that particular school. Administrators were particularly pleased if the candidate selected by the committee and the candidate recommended by the administrator were the same person, but the administrators were willing to select a different person if they felt the teacher brought a special talent and quality needed in the school.

Superintendents wanted to be in a position with their boards to be able to make specific recommendations about naming new school principals and other administrators. In a number of larger school districts, superintendents indicated that a number of other individuals in the system provided initial screening of new candidates but the superintendent made the final recommendation to the board. In very few instances did superintendents say their boards refused to honor those recommendations.

In reviewing the characteristics of the superintendents in question, they recognized the sensitive process for recommending new employees, since many of them would not necessarily be coming from within the district. Where there was the least consternation about hiring "outsiders," we found, districts had gone on record with a board-approved policy of hiring the best candidates. In many cases, objective interviewing techniques helped to substantiate the qualities and characteristics of those recommended for hiring. Where the policy was less clear or nonexistent, some superintendents did have to defer to the board in large measure. The very best superintendents were clear in their policy decisions and hiring recommendations.

Too often school administrators have to make hiring decisions based on application materials that do not give proper attention to the candidate. In many instances these weak applications ask for the standard demographic and certification information. They usually ask for a list of experiences in chronological order and usually ask for at least three references. Interspersed with these questions will be one asking candidates to discuss their philosophy, their greatest strength or weakness, and why they would like to teach in this particular district.

In the better districts, applications also will garner information about how teachers understand and implement effective schools research. They will want specific information about how a teacher ensures that learning is taking place in the class, how well all the students are doing, and how they can document and communicate student progress.

Even if a candidate has no teaching experience, the best prospects will explain how they would behave if they were a teacher or had teaching experience. The less competent might say that since they have no teaching experience, they cannot fully address the question. The best administrators are leery of hiring the latter candidates.

The best administrators do something in the hiring process that only the best do: They check references. They also check beyond the references. The real problem with references is that no candidate will intentionally list negative references. Thus a superior administrator will ask specific questions about a candidate's character or teaching experience to elicit information that can help predict success. For example, some teachers talk about watching children grow. The better candidates discuss how intricately they want to be involved with the growth and development of their students and can give specific examples of how they have done this. If they have no experience, they may preface their remarks by saying, "If I were a teacher . . . " and answer the question basically the same way, and formulating a response similar to that of the best teacher candidates.

The best administrators know the professional tendencies of the prospective candidates. They may check with parents of students in the previous school; they may check with support personal, community leaders, and PTA members, along with homeroom mothers and volunteers. The important thing, however, is that they will check the backgrounds and have a good picture of how the teacher or candidate has performed or probably will perform in the district.

With the current trend toward litigation, it is increasingly difficult to get straightforward responses about candidates because many people who give references are concerned about law suits over negative comments. Unfortunately, teachers and administrators who have been less than effective may receive positive recommendations so they can be removed from the district. Their ineffectiveness now becomes a problem for the receiving district. *Caveat emptor.*

As with any profession, the bell curve stratifies professional educators. About 6 to 8 percent of teachers or administrators will be superior. If districts want to identify superior professionals, they need a policy that underpins the process, since the selection procedures will tend to be more comprehensive, and in some cases expensive, if indistrict visitations are implemented.

Better teachers, administrators, and employees making a substantial contribution to the improved culture of the school or district will be the "return on investment" for identifying the best candidates. Districts should, therefore, select the best people. A good policy can reduce the concern for hiring outside the district. This is not to minimize the normal pressures to hire from within. Good judgment is critical to support staff morale, and there must be a balance of internal and external candidates. Continual high-quality professional growth and inservice opportunities can give good support to internal candidates and district employees. Professional growth must be more than a "dartboard game" with teachers and administrators taking their best shot at what to offer as skills development programs.

Administrators need to be such good instructional leaders that they can identify those areas where support for growth is needed. These same administrators, however, will be accentuating the outstanding characteristics of the teachers and enabling teachers to grow and develop. If the district builds an excellent staff development program, the level of competence will be increased. If an outside candidate is hired, ultimately he or she will have to be equal or superior to the internal candidate to win the position. Who wins, really? The board of education, the parents, the community, the students, and the rest of the staff. A great school district develops a rich tapestry of professionals from throughout the country to add their design to the mix.

Too often candidates are selected from the same colleges or universities in the state. In many cases the superintendents and principals received their degrees from these same institutions. There is some precedent for selecting from the same campuses. However, there is a point at which too many candidates can come from the same philosophy.

Districts that are small, rural, or otherwise not inclined to attract a wide variety of candidates from throughout the country will obviously need to choose from among the best candidates who do apply regardless where they live. Several administrators indicated that if they were not satisfied with the quality of the applicants, they would fill the position with substitutes until they could attract the best candidate. Conversely, several administrators also indicated that if they found a top-notch candidate, they would create a position for the individual to secure his or her employment until the appropriate position opened. In this case, the administrators knew they had found superior talent. If they did not find a place for the individual, that person would probably take another position outside the recruiting district.

Outstanding administrators hire the best talent they can find. It is their best insurance for developing a superior school district. They look for candidates with superior communication skills, high sensitivity and expectations, and willingness to take calculated risks to serve students better. They look for confident, creative candidates who help students and adults exceed their own expectations. They look for big dreamers and big thinkers who expect big results and who push themselves beyond their mental models of excellence.

In districts that hire positive, progressive professionals, look for eager student learners, higher student test scores, lower professional turnover, good school-parent-community relations, a supportive environment where students stay in school through graduation. By combining vision with a "can-do" attitude, there really is no limit to the good districts can accomplish.

11

PERSONAL DEVELOPMENT AND PROFESSIONAL ORGANIZATIONS

What makes you think you are a good administrator? Are you a great leader? Can you be as effective and successful in a larger environment as you are now? These are the questions each of us needs to answer. For some, the answer has come from a general, personal chronicle of observations about effectiveness on the job and perhaps some feedback from fellow administrators, teachers, students, and parents or citizens. For others, the answer has come from a more objective source—from personal development workshops and seminars to success in reaching leadership positions within state and national professional organizations and associations.

A majority of administrators in this study connected their personal development and their professional development from affiliation with professional organizations. By combining the themes of school leaders, these two contributors to administrators' successes fit together logically and make easy reading.

What can we say about personal development? That it is a major discriminator in separating exceptional administrators from the average? That it underpins a lifestyle by which outstanding administrators live? That it provides benchmarks by which outstanding administrators can identify their strengths and vulnerabilities so they can map a continuous program of improvement? A resounding yes to each of the questions.

Personal development and a sincere willingness to give personal time to and take skill improvements from professional associations are two powerful ways to get on the fast track to exceptional performance. Administrators who discussed their commitment to personal skill development had an objective assessment of their strengths and weaknesses, were willing to discuss them openly, and had designed strategies to minimize their weaknesses either by remediation or by surrounding themselves with skilled individuals who complemented their vulnerabilities. In either case, these individuals had a good sense of their abilities and reported feeling good about what they could contribute to the success of their organizations.

Administrators who participated in this study, including those who are not quoted in this book, recognized and appreciated the hard work it took to become successful. Some humbly insisted they were in the right place at the right time; others were quick to attribute their success to other people; still others expressed surprise that they had been singled out by their professional peers as highly successful administrators in their states. In virtually every case, these same administrators talked about a lifetime of thought, effort, and refinement that went into the development of their leadership abilities and the successes they have had as a result of implementing those abilities.

They seemed to echo a hand-painted sign in a training center for junior athletes in a Virginia school, "The only place where success comes before work is in the dictionary." Work alone, however, does not always lead to administrative success. As Gerhard Gschwandtner stated in his book *$uperachiever$* (1984, 3), "Before you can begin working toward success, you need to (1) define what success means to you, and (2) decide on the action steps leading to success."

James Kouzes, CEO of TPG Learning Systems, Palo Alto, California, says that small-business leaders can leverage their position by building their credibility. His research identifies four major characteristics people look for in their leaders: honesty, a forward focus, the ability to inspire, and competence: "Honesty, integrity, ethical behavior, and trustworthiness is the key ingredient in the leadership brew" (*Industry Week,* June 20, 1994, 22). In Kouzes' work, honesty has consistently been the single most identified characteristic of effective leadership.

To a great extent, self-knowledge is a primary concern and interest for those administrators who really have an overriding desire to be effective and successful. Self-knowledge connotes knowing the truth about yourself. When an affiliate of the NASSP Principals' Assessment Center was established at the University of Nebraska-Lincoln, a segment of the school administrators at all levels enrolled in the program; many became certified assessors. Initially there was overwhelming support for the process, procedures, and feedback.

Something interesting happened, however, after several years of successful operation: Fewer administrators signed up for the experience or the training. In reviewing the enrollment data, the first administrators in the program nearly all had a positive concept of their leadership effectiveness. The program subsequently documented and substantiated what they sensed was their effectiveness. The participants were administrators who could take that information and capitalize on it. They were not intimidated by an honest appraisal of their skills.

As the years progressed, however, the decline in the participation rate increased. Could a case be built that administrators who did not sign up for the original programs may have had reservations about their abilities and what the Assessment Center would uncover? Were they less sure of their leadership abilities and less likely to want to see an honest appraisal of their skills?

The point in mentioning these data is not to build a case for the declining use of the Assessment Center but to realize that successful administrators indicate a willingness to participate in and review self-assessment opportunities as avenues to learn more about themselves, know where they are strong, design strategies to minimize their vulnerabilities, and generally continue to put themselves in positions where they can exert the most leadership.

Great leaders think past the daily routines and envision a better future. Maintaining a forward focus, using one's actions to move the organization toward the future, requires more than a vision, a formal mission statement, and a strategic plan. It is a state of mind, say Doug Krug and Ed Oakley, co-authors of *Enlightened Leadership: Getting to the Heart of Change* (1993). They recommend that forward thinking be a daily activity of leaders.

Former North Carolina Senator Sam Ervin, Jr., described a leader as someone who "wants power not for himself but in order to be of service. I think a good leader exercises power to improve the lot of other people or to improve a system" (*$uperachiever$*, Gschwandtner, 1984, 150).

Too often, administrators get caught up in so many routine details that they fail to make time to contemplate changes, movements, and innovations in the profession. A primary value of joining and supporting a professional organization to enhance leadership is the opportunity to exchange ideas of complex issues facing education on a larger scale. It is easy for administrators to become so mesmerized by what is going on around them in their school districts that they miss the events on the larger screen. School leaders need to be aware of significant events and potential policy issues on the horizon, to be able to connect with individuals who have studied the issues, to give valuable insights into their solution, and to increase networking with individuals who can help shape thinking about these issues. Professional development activities and interaction with professional association members serve as two ideal ways to move leadership and influence ahead.

THE EDUCATION NETWORK

No school administrators responding to this study indicated they could do the job by themselves. In many cases they referred to the larger network of individuals who became role models for them and helped clarify issues and techniques that would enhance their leadership potential.

A director of elementary education in Texas, said that her thirty-plus years in public education had enabled her to be a service for childrens' educational needs— elementary through high school. If she was considered an outstanding educator, it was in part because professional organizations had kept her an ever-inspired learner of her craft. Serving as an officer of the Texas Elementary Principal and Supervisor Association (TEPSA), applying learned skills and techniques through a wealth of interactions with peers, and sharing and caring for fellow professionals through Phi Delta Kappa involvements had kept her professionally at the front line. Many outstanding Texas educators were her professional and personal friends. Their support of her, of her career aspirations, and of her endeavors lifted each professional project, goal, and objective to a new level in her career.

A high school principal in South Carolina listed important characteristics of successful and happy teachers. She is serious but does not take herself too seriously; she is effective, but not domineering; proud but not egotistical.

She said students were the important people in her business. She must be an advocate for students. She must take risks for students and on behalf of improved student learning. She must maintain integrity in all that she does. She must work harder than her staff. She must maintain high expectations for all, including herself. She must treat all people in a fair, caring way. She must care about her own professional development and the professional development of staff. She must build leadership in the people with whom she works. She must be tolerant of others' views and opinions and open to compromise, but she must never sacrifice her principles and values. She must be a leader and a team player. She must be open to change and help to create a climate for change in the school. She must maintain a healthy sense of self and a "gigantic" sense of humor.

She must take her business seriously, but not take herself too seriously. This advice was followed literally when she was on her way to a meeting to address a group concerning the needs of at-risk students and looked down to notice that she had on one blue shoe and one black shoe.

She noted that effective schools are reasonably happy places to be. They are places where folks remember that education is a people business; where those in charge are willing to take risks for the good of those who aren't; where the doors are open to community, to bright ideas, or even to dumb notions . . . where the teachers are serious about teaching and learning but don't take themselves too seriously; where everyone feels some success but always wants to do better; where everybody knows who is in charge, but where everybody's opinion counts; where job descriptions or course outlines don't stop peoples' imaginations and creative efforts; where federal guidelines, state mandates, and district policies are respected but not permitted to impede what it is educators are all about; where the pride in a proud past does not become an obstacle to a bright future.

Is professional development something that ends? Is it possible to spend sufficient time or take sufficient courses to "have arrived"? Not according to a superintendent in Missouri. No matter how good the school system, the administrators, or whatever is being considered, it can always be better." We never "arrive." We are always on a path toward improvement, he believed. He could not imagine thinking of himself or a school system with which he was involved as being as good as it can be.

If a district or administrator really believes individuals can be better and provide better educational opportunities for students, how does the district practice what it preaches? For Les Anderson (personal communication, October 14, 1991), a middle school principal in North Dakota, professional development is a goal established for himself and in partnership with teachers.

The staff are encouraged to use the latest in curriculum and technology and in some cases as part of their professional goals. The staff at the middle school are expected to travel professionally at district expense and report information back to the entire staff. All staff are expected to be involved in staff development.

All staff are involved in professional growth activities that are part of the evaluation process. The principal and the teacher cooperatively set instructional goals at the beginning of each school term. The goals focus on what the teacher is going to do instructionally that is different or better than in the past.

Should you go out on a limb for your professional beliefs about public education? As a school administrator, how can becoming a high-profile person enhance the school programs or the school district?

Jim Buchanan (personal communication, December 3, 1991), a superintendent for a Phoenix, Arizona, high school district, has maintained a high profile in a number of states where he has been a school leader. He has been an active team player with his professional associations, as well as an advocate for public education, addressing groups and organizations influential in their support of public education.

I am outgoing and gregarious by nature, so it is easy for me to engage in high-profile activities. For example, I always accept invitations to present at or to participate in the planning of state and national conferences. I attempt to serve my state association in whatever fashion I can and am particularly active in the legislative arena. I prepare and deliver testimony at public hearings and attempt to establish personal relationships with legislators, office holders, and business leaders. The local chamber of commerce is an excellent avenue, since these folks are always looking for people to participate in chamber activities. Chambers typically have legislative affairs committees and are usually receptive to having educational leaders serve on these committees, since state budgets have large segments of educational funding. I try to assume roles in local service clubs that sponsor communitywide projects. Ultimately, an educational leader must find every possible opportunity to further the public education agenda locally, statewide, and nationally. Maintaining a high profile enables me to take advantage of more of these opportunities.

Outstanding administrators know and value the technique of networking. They talk with individuals they want to meet who have information that might be useful to them. Networking is a technique for determining whom they need to visit and finding someone who knows that individual well enough to enable contact. The value of networking is that usually the person suggesting the network contact will either call the acquaintance and tell him or her that the administrator will be calling or the person will give permission to use his or her name as an introduction when the contact is initiated.

Seventy percent of the jobs in this country are found through networking. It is the most productive method for linking with a source of information that individuals have determined will be valuable to them. Since this is the fastest way for people to get the information they need, networking should be part of successful administrators' professional growth plans.

See how the next three administrators focus on networking but with a different twist in each case. First, Michael Burk (personal communication, February 18, 1992), assistant principal for a high school in West Virginia:

> The greatest influence on my professional maturity came from talking and listening and learning from active school administrators. It made little difference how similar our schools were; I always seemed to pick up another professional building block from their experiences. Although literature, like the *NASSP Bulletin*, provided valuable data, I seemed to get more out of personal conversations with principals. It is my opinion that you also value actual experience, as is indicated by the nature of your request for information.
>
> If you see, hear, or read about an educational operation you think might work in your school, use it. The collective imagination that went into the operation, plus your adaptation to fit your environment, saves many mental hours of working out the logistics. This was helpful in my influence on the school district's decisions about computer assistance with administrative logistics.
>
> I participate conscientiously in our state professional organization. This is where I get large quantities of valuable information to enhance my professional orientation and development. The rewards of this peer interaction have been extremely valuable to me.
>
> I try to read professional and business literature. The NASSP literature provides the professional input while educational authors provide the educational business input. Also I rely on motivational speakers (i.e., Lou Holtz, Zig Ziglar) to keep me on track to strive for success.

A high school principal in Kansas looked at networking as a catalyst for professional growth. He was willing to continue to learn and grow professionally. He had not found a single technique or program that would cure all the problems. Therefore, he was open to all ideas that would help him develop a variety of solutions to educational problems. This meant he read all he could read, attended as many conferences, seminars, and workshops as he could, and picked his colleagues' brains as much as he could.

Jim Buchanan (personal communication, December 3, 1991) explains how he uses networking for information and advice.

> There simply is too much to know in the education business for any one person to know everything. I realized this very early in my career and proceeded to create a network of informal advisors to whom I could turn

for help and advice. Most people appreciate being asked for their advice, so it is not difficult to encourage people to serve in such a role. Having been educated in Nebraska, I found it easy to identify those within the state who would be valuable advisors by simply asking my professors and supervisors who would be a good source of this type of information or who has these skills, and so on. As I moved to other states, I was able to uncover the same types of people and thereby broadened my network. I became involved in AASA and expanded my network on a national level via AASA staff and committee members. I use state and national conferences periodically to maintain contact with network members as well as correspond on an as-needed basis.

A special education director in South Dakota shares her time to get valuable information. She spends a great deal of energy using her skills and interests to help community and professional organizations in her community and state. Professional involvement and commitment is important. It gives her contact with other professionals who can give her ideas and support, and it challenges her to prepare and to share ideas and skills.

A high school principal in Connecticut said he was involved relatively extensively in professional associations, including the state school association's Principals Academy and a variety of community-level groups. This expanded his horizons and provided opportunities not only to contribute to education in a more generous sense but also to have a better sense of what was transpiring in the overall community.

A high school principal in Montana reflected on her early years in the profession. Looking back through the years, she recognized that she had listened to many senior administrators. She used their ideas and practices and modified others to fit her situation. She became involved in the MASSP/NASSP early in her career and met some great administrators.

A junior-senior high school principal in Alaska stays involved in her associations despite the geographic challenges. She states it is important to be highly involved in professional activities. She makes sure she is an active participant in her district, state, and national professional organizations (i.e., AASSP, NASSP, ASCD, chamber of commerce, etc.). This involvement is evidenced by her being an officer, committee member, mentor, writer for newsletters, and presenter at state conferences.

Ken Bird (personal communication, November 29, 1991), is a superintendent in one of the most progressive school districts in Nebraska. His ability to develop and to use networks has been a key to his success.

A fundamental conviction I hold is that being a part of a network of successful professionals will enhance the likelihood of my being successful. I believe there is nothing profound about this conviction. It is simply a behavior I have found that helps bring out the best in me.

Networks of friends, both personal and professional, are an important aspect of a successful administrator's career. Successful administrators must take responsibility for their own development, and this development should include support networks.

Administrators who have participated in workshops and seminars have indicated on evaluation forms that one of the most important aspects of the program was the opportunity to network with other administrators. In the time spent away from workshops during breaks, over meals, or in the evening, administrators have visited with others and shared experience, traded ideas, and developed support networks that may continue throughout their careers.

As suggested by respondents, many administrators knew early in their careers that networking with professional and business organizations would give them good contacts, insights, and suggestions that could be molded to fit their particular school or district challenges.

Too often in looking at networking as a method of identifying people who can help, administrators sometimes make the mistake of thinking that they are asking a favor of their network contact and should therefore use networking on a limited basis or not at all. Networking is not asking people for a favor; it is asking people for advice. Since most people are flattered when someone asks them for their advice, don't let this important method of getting and giving information slip from your repertoire of techniques for acquiring valuable management and leadership information.

David Haney (personal communication, March 9, 1992), assistant superintendent in Jamestown, North Dakota, in his second response to this study said:

When I made the comment that I set goals for myself and measure them on a regular basis, I was referring to a specific procedure I follow. I have taken my job description and broken it into tasks. For each task, I have written an objective. The objectives are placed in a tickler file. Every Friday morning I evaluate on a scale of one (low) to three (high) my performance in meeting the objectives established for that week. When my self-evaluation scale indicates that my performance was not effective, I either redo the project or write a new objective to assure that I will do a better job the next time the task has to be done.

When I said I dedicate time and talent to being effective, I mean that I make a conscious effort to improve. For example, one of my responsibilities is to evaluate the principals. I did not feel I was providing them with appropriate guidance. I found the solution to my problem by completing the NASSP Principals' Assessment training program. I used vacation time to complete the training rather than take personal leave.

A high school principal in Ohio stated that it is important to a successful principal to attend workshops, conferences, and conventions, to hear his or her peers bring forth creative ideas in successful administration. He said we need to get out into the field, rub elbows, and hear what's happening. It is very easy to become stagnant in our environment and forget that the same problems are occurring to other principals on a daily basis. Exchanging experiences and certain scenarios are very important at a conference, and much can be learned by listening. He said it is imperative, whether at the local, state, or national level, that building administrators attend meetings where they can mix with fellow administrators. These exchanges always reinforce what educators are doing, or they spur creative thinking for change. Administrators use conferences and workshops to improve their productivity.

A superintendent in North Dakota wrote that he is a real believer in the fact that school administrators must lead by example. He spends many hours on the job beyond what is required. Administrators must model the level of energy, the attitude, and the commitment they expect from their employees. He has always had a positive attitude and a lot of pride in accomplishment—two traits he thinks are essential to a successful school administrator. Continued training and the association with colleagues who are the most successful also have contributed to his administrative success. He likes to determine who is the most successful and then spend time with that person to determine what he would need to do to polish his skills in that area.

An assistant superintendent in Washington State remarked she believes that as a successful administrator, she needs to model the importance of personal and professional growth by taking classes, presenting at workshops and so on. Moving outside of existing paradigms is crucial, and her focus is on continuing education. Personal growth and development allows this paradigm shift to occur.

Successful administrators know the value of continuous professional improvement. They offer no excuses for looking for additional ways to improve their leadership effectiveness. For many, joining, working, and supporting professional associations gives them the exposure to issues and the networking capability to keep them on the leading edge of educational improvements and personal accomplishments.

REFERENCES

Gschwandtner, Gerhard. (1984). *$uperachiever$*. Englewood Cliffs, NJ: Prentice-Hall.

Krug, Doug, & Oakley, Ed. (1993). *Enlightened Leadership: Getting to the Heart of Change*. New York: Simon & Schuster.

INDEX

About the Authors

FREDERICK C. WENDEL is Professor of Educational Administration at the University of Nebraska-Lincoln.

FRED A. HOKE has served on the Ohio County Board of Education in Wheeling, West Virginia, and in the West Virginia School Boards Association in Charleston. He owns a consulting business in education policy promotion and personal skills development.

RONALD G. JOEKEL is Executive Director of Phi Delta Kappa International. Formerly, he was Professor and Chair of the Department of Educational Administration, Associate Professor of Curriculum and Instruction, and Associate Dean of Teachers College, University of Nebraska-Lincoln.

ISBN 0-275-94822-6

9 780275 948221

HARDCOVER BAR CODE